LEARN
ROCK CLIMBING
IN A WEEKEND

LEARN
ROCK CLIMBING
IN A WEEKEND

KEVIN WALKER

Photography by Peter Chadwick

DORLING KINDERSLEY
London • New York • Stuttgart

A DORLING KINDERSLEY BOOK

Art Editor Tracy Hambleton
Senior Art Editor Tina Vaughan
Project Editor Ann Kay
Series Editor James Harrison
Senior Editor Sean Moore
Production Controller Meryl Silbert

First published in Great Britain in 1991
by Dorling Kindersley Limited,
9 Henrietta Street, London WC2E 8PS

A CIP catalogue record for this book is available from the British Library

ISBN 0-86318-663-7

Computer page make-up by The Cooling Brown Partnership
Reproduced by Colourscan, Singapore
Printed and bound by Arnoldo Mondadori, Verona, Italy

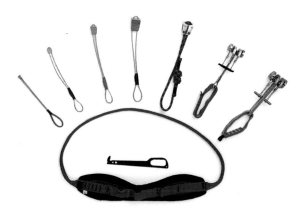

CONTENTS

Introduction 6

PREPARING FOR THE WEEKEND 8

Features of a rockface 10
Climbing clothing................12
A firm footing......................14
Personal safety 16
Basic equipment 18
Packs & protection 20

The right ropes 22
Know your knots.................24
Approaches to climbing.......26
Grading systems and
 guidebooks.......................32
Climbing calls 34

THE WEEKEND COURSE 36

Day 1

Learning the ropes 38
Tying on 40
Fixing anchors.....................42

Belaying...............................44
Using basic holds................50
First moves..........................52

Day 2

Moving on 58
Overcoming obstacles 60
Abseiling 70

Multi-pitch climbing...........74
Taking the lead....................76
Self-help..............................80

AFTER THE WEEKEND 84

Where to climb 86

The mountain code.............90

Glossary 92
Index 94
Acknowledgments 96
Getting in touch 96

INTRODUCTION

AT ITS BEST, ROCK CLIMBING is exhilarating, challenging, healthy, and fun – an activity unlike any other. When approached in the correct way, it is also nowhere near as dangerous as many people think. Thanks to the development of modern safety equipment, climbing routes that would have been considered dangerous ten years ago can now be done with relative security.

It is important to understand the difference between rock climbing and mountaineering. Rock climbing is concerned simply with movement on rock, although a little "mountaincraft" may be needed to reach the more remote crags. Mountaineering – of which rock climbing is an important part – also involves movement on snow and ice, glaciers, steep grass, scree, and suchlike. Although many climbers are also keen mountaineers, a growing number of "rock gymnasts" concern themselves exclusively with rock climbing.

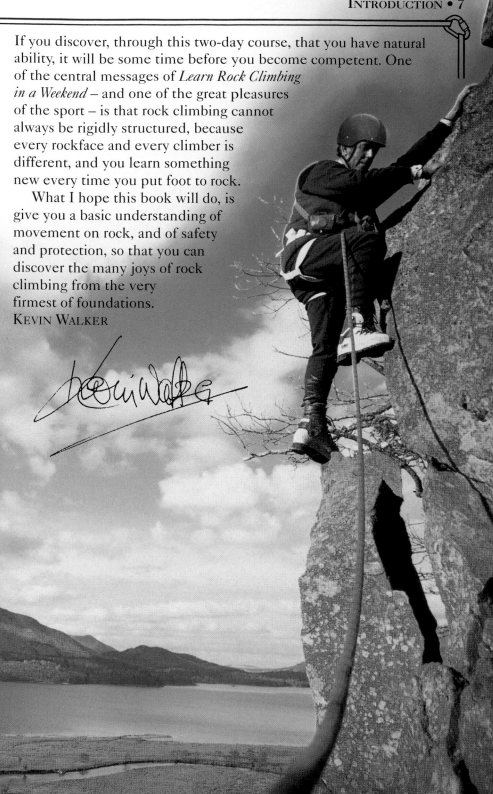

If you discover, through this two-day course, that you have natural ability, it will be some time before you become competent. One of the central messages of *Learn Rock Climbing in a Weekend* – and one of the great pleasures of the sport – is that rock climbing cannot always be rigidly structured, because every rockface and every climber is different, and you learn something new every time you put foot to rock.

What I hope this book will do, is give you a basic understanding of movement on rock, and of safety and protection, so that you can discover the many joys of rock climbing from the very firmest of foundations.

KEVIN WALKER

PREPARING FOR THE WEEKEND

Gain maximum benefit from your weekend by planning in advance

ROCK CLIMBING IS NOT ONLY fairly weather-dependent, it can also be quite painful for novices who rush in without some prior thought! To get the most from these two days, choose a time of year when you have the best chance of warm, sunny weather, and try to visit an area that has several different crags, offering a wide variety of easy climbs.

BOOTS
Your footwear is vitally important. You don't need to buy expensive rock boots, but you will need good-quality trainers or walking boots (pp.14-15).

EQUIPMENT
Learn to recognize the equipment (pp.18-19) by visiting a climbing shop.

Protection devices

Karabiner **Belay** *plate*

PROTECTION
Get to know the basic safety equipment and procedures.

KNOTS
Learn to tie the basic knots with your eyes closed (pp.24-25).

Teaching yourself rock climbing is not to be recommended. Mistakes can be painful, and, if you do get it wrong and fall off from any height, you could be seriously injured. For this reason, it is best if you can spend your weekend with an experienced companion who has been climbing for several years and has his or her own equipment. Ask them if they are willing to take you slowly through the various skills and demonstrate how different obstacles are overcome. Climbing equipment cannot usually be hired, so ask whether your companion will lend you the basic personal kit of harness and helmet.

*Words in **bold** are given a further explanation in the glossary (p.92).*

HARNESS
A climbing harness enables you to experiment with harder moves in relative safety (pp.16-17).

BAGS
It's worth taking a proper rucksack in which to carry your **gear**, spare clothing, food and drink, and a small first aid kit (p.20).

FEATURES OF A ROCKFACE

Identifying the different characteristics of the rockface

YOU MAY BE BAFFLED the first time you read a climbing guidebook. The route descriptions will contain a complete language of unfamiliar terms. Some refer to climbing technique, but others, such as **overlap** and **chimney**, describe specific rockface features.

OVERLAP •
This term is commonly used for a small **overhang**, although true **overlaps** are formed where one layer of rock is displaced in relation to its neighbour.

RIDGE •
Often used synonymously with "arête", "ridge" can also refer to a shallow, linear projection from the main rockface.

CORNER •
In rock climbing, "corner" usually refers to a wide, "open book" type of feature with an angle of between about 60° and 120° between the faces. Where the angle is less than 60°, the feature is usually called an "open chimney"; where it is over 120°, a "groove" (see opposite page).

NOSE •
A nose is, quite simply, a local protuberance – a prow of rock that juts out from the main body of the cliff. Although sometimes climbed over, it is often possible to detour around them.

ARETE •
The opposite of a corner, arêtes often provide exposed and exhilarating climbing. On mountain crags, they may be long and rambling; some may even be knife-edged.

LEDGE •
This is self-explanatory. A **mantelshelf** is an isolated ledge.

GETTING TO KNOW THE ROCKFACE

STUDYING THE FEATURES

Whenever you go climbing, it is a good idea to study the rockface from some distance away, as you will be able to identify many more features than you can when close up. This enables you to plan out your chosen climb with much less difficulty, especially if the base of the cliff is hidden in trees or vegetation. Route finding can be difficult on mountain crags, and you will find that a general overview of the cliff is extremely useful.

CAPTURING THE MOOD

Most good climbs follow definite features – a wall, an arête, a corner, and so on. Each feature gives a different type of climbing, and you must learn to judge the type of climbing from the features involved in the route. The combination of features also affects the atmosphere of a rockface – a north-facing crag with damp **chimneys** and forbidding **overhangs** is an altogether more sombre place than a south-facing cliff with warm walls and sunny ridges.

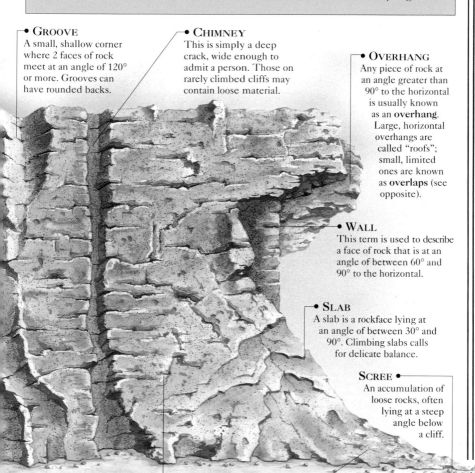

• GROOVE
A small, shallow corner where 2 faces of rock meet at an angle of 120° or more. Grooves can have rounded backs.

• CHIMNEY
This is simply a deep crack, wide enough to admit a person. Those on rarely climbed cliffs may contain loose material.

• OVERHANG
Any piece of rock at an angle greater than 90° to the horizontal is usually known as an **overhang**. Large, horizontal overhangs are called "roofs"; small, limited ones are known as **overlaps** (see opposite).

• WALL
This term is used to describe a face of rock that is at an angle of between 60° and 90° to the horizontal.

• SLAB
A slab is a rockface lying at an angle of between 30° and 90°. Climbing slabs calls for delicate balance.

SCREE •
An accumulation of loose rocks, often lying at a steep angle below a cliff.

CRACK •
Another self-explanatory term. Cracks that are wider than a human fist are often called "off-widths".

GLACIS •
A glacis is a face of rock lying at an angle of up to 30° to the horizontal.

CLIMBING CLOTHING

How to dress for comfort and safety

TO GET THE MOST out of climbing, you need comfortable clothes. On warm days at valley sites, the experienced climber usually wears a running vest and climbing tights, but a T-shirt and stretchy tracksuit bottoms are equally suitable. For cooler weather, a warm tracksuit is ideal, and a fleece jacket is a useful standby at most times of the year. Take tough gloves for **belaying** (see pp.44-49), but don't wear them when climbing, as they prevent you from gaining a good grip. When going to a mountain crag, always take extra clothing that is warm and windproof, as well as a full set of waterproofs.

VEST
As a beginner, you will tend to get hot easily because you will use your arm muscles more than is really necessary. This makes a running vest or T-shirt the best choice for warmer weather. You will also be placing your arms in all kinds of unusual positions, and a vest or T-shirt allows freedom of movement.

CLIMBING TIGHTS
Generally made of stretchy Lycra, and surprisingly warm, climbing tights are usually brightly coloured. Their main advantage is that they do not restrict your leg movement.

Footloops stop legs from riding up and impeding movement

A large collar will keep your neck warm

Strong, full-length zip

High, elasticated waistband that fits snugly above your hips

TROUSERS
Stretchy tracksuit bottoms are a good alternative to climbing tights. As you may need to bend or stretch into quite extreme positions, your clothing mustn't restrict movement. You also need to see your feet, so ensure that your trouser legs aren't baggy.

Leather palms

FLEECE JACKET
A fleece jacket is useful if the weather turns cool, and you will be surprised how windproof some of the thinner fleece materials can be. Your jacket needs to be long enough to cover the top of your buttocks, and roomy enough not to hamper movement. Inner, zipped pockets are useful for keeping any small items – such as car keys and coins – safe.

GLOVES
You will need a pair of tough gloves to prevent possible rope burn when you are **belaying** (see pp.44-49). An old pair of gardening gloves is ideal. Don't wear them while climbing.

A FIRM FOOTING

Selecting the right footwear makes all the difference

IT IS NOT ESSENTIAL FOR BEGINNERS to buy specialist rock boots – good trainers or walking boots are fine. Indeed, these types of footwear force you to place your feet correctly on holds, helping you to develop a good technique from the start. Rock boots allow you to get away with sloppy technique on easier climbs, which can lead to problems later on. Ensure that your footwear is as comfortable as possible, and a good fit. Whatever type you choose, avoid climbing on wet or icy rock.

WALKING BOOTS

These are essential for walking to the more remote mountain crags, especially if the weather is wet. Lightweight hill-walking boots are also perfectly adequate for easier rock climbs.

• SOCKS
You will need a pair of thick socks to wear with your walking boots. Choose ones made of wool, with thick, loopstitch soles.

SOLE •
The sole of the boot should be fairly rigid, to protect the base of the foot. It should also have a good, deep tread pattern.

• ANKLE SUPPORT
While protecting the base of your feet and giving you a good grip, boots must also provide adequate support for your ankles.

TRAINERS

Trainers are an acceptable substitute for rock boots when starting out, although they won't cope well with muddy paths on the walk to the rockface.

THE INSIDE STORY
Wear thin socks inside your trainers. These enable you to "feel" the holds better.

TOE
Trainers in which the sole is flat for its entire length are far better on small holds than those in which the sole is angled upwards at the toe.

SOLE •
The best trainers are those that have a substantial sole, and that offer good support to the entire foot. The stiffer they are, the better. Choose trainers with rubber, rather than plastic, soles.

TAKING CARE
Make sure your footwear is in good condition before you set out for your climb. Check the laces for any signs of damage, and replace them where necessary.

ROCK BOOTS

When it comes to rock-climbing footwear, rock boots represent the "state of the art". They are ideal for harder climbs with smaller footholds, because they offer excellent friction and allow you to "feel" the holds. They are worn very tight, which means they are not renowned for comfort!

GOING BAREFOOT
Because they are designed to be worn tight, many climbers do not wear socks inside rock boots.

TOE •
The toe of the boot is as narrow as possible. This design enables you to **jam** your foot right into extremely thin cracks in the rockface.

SOLE •
Rock boots have flat soles made from "sticky" butyl rubber. This must be kept scrupulously clean to guarantee maximum efficiency.

HEEL •
The "rand", which runs around the boot, extends upwards at the heel, offering good friction when "heel hooking" (see pp.68-69).

PERSONAL SAFETY

What to look for in climbing helmets and harnesses

•

YOU CAN CLIMB LOW BOULDERS or try low-level **traversing** (see pp.52-53) as soon as you have suitable clothing and footwear. However, if you want to gain any height, you must wear a helmet, and you will also need the security of a rope. Rather than tying the rope around your waist, it is safer, and more comfortable, to wear a belt or harness.

HELMETS

You must choose a helmet that is specifically designed for climbing. There are 2 main types of helmet currently available – standard and lightweight. Lightweight helmets do not protect the head as well as standard ones. An integral part of the structure of both kinds of helmet is the internal framework, called a cradle, which is usually adjustable over a range of head sizes.

STANDARD HELMET
Standard climbing helmets have strong, fibreglass shells with shock-absorbent foam linings. The substantial, Y-shaped chin strap is attached extremely firmly to the internal cradle at 4 points, which means that the helmet will stay firmly on the head despite blows from any direction.

LIGHTWEIGHT HELMET
While many climbers prefer the comfort of lightweight helmets, they offer less protection than standard ones. The basic design is the same as for standard helmets, but the shells are often made from other materials such as polycarbonate and thermo-plastic, and, in the most expensive models, from carbon fibres.

HARNESS AND BELT

To attach your climbing rope for safety and comfort, choose a climbing belt or a sit harness. Both belts and harnesses are designed to spread the load in the event of a fall. A sit harness is really preferable to a belt, and is absolutely essential if you intend to do any **lead climbing**.

SIT HARNESS

Gear loop

Wide, padded waist belt

Buckle

Belay (rope tie-on) loop

Leg loop

CLIMBER'S BELT

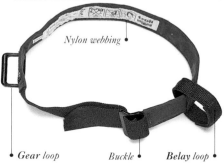

Nylon webbing

Gear *loop*

Buckle

Belay *loop*

PARTS
A sit harness consists of 2 parts: a waist belt, and leg loops. These are permanently connected in some models.

PARTS
A climber's belt is a length of wide, nylon webbing that is secured around the waist by a locking buckle.

LEG LOOPS
These take less load than the belt, but ensure that a fallen climber will hang in a seated position, and not from the waist.

WAIST BELTS
Climbers' belts, and the waist belts of harnesses, are made from strong, wide, nylon webbing that spreads the load of a fall over a large area. They should fit snugly above the hips.

BELT SAFETY
As with the sit harness, it is vital that the buckle of your belt is always fastened correctly (see p.41).

BASIC EQUIPMENT

*What **gear** does the modern climber need?*

TAPES, "KRABS", CHOCKS, WIRES ... all part of the jargon
of rock climbing. In the event of a fall, it is technical
climbing equipment such as this that may well prevent
injury. It is, therefore, important to use the best you can
afford, and to understand exactly what each piece of
equipment is designed to do. Although much will become
apparent as you progress, it is useful to understand some
basics before you start. In addition to reading as much as
possible about climbing, a visit to a good climbing
equipment shop run by enthusiasts is recommended.

TAPE SLINGS
Tape **slings**, or "tapes", are
lengths of strong, nylon webbing
that are sewn into slings using bar
tacking or similar (not a job to do
yourself). They are available, in
order of increasing strength, in
standard tape, tubular tape, super
tape, and super tube. Tapes
come in a variety of widths –
usually 15mm (½in), 19mm (¾in),
and 25mm (1in) – and a number
of standard lengths. They have
many uses, for example, placing
around small rock pinnacles, or
extending **protection** devices
(see pp.21, 42-43, and 78-79).

• STANDARD SLING
Made from super tape and 120cm
(4ft) long, this has a breaking strain
of around 2.5 tonnes (2½ tons).

• LONG SLING
The longest standard length of sewn
sling is 240cm (8ft). This is useful for
belays, and can be used double.

KARABINERS

Often called "krabs", these metal snaplinks, with sprung opening gates, are used as connections between a range of climbing equipment. Made of steel, or less hard-wearing aluminium alloy, they come in various shapes and sizes. Alloy **karabiners** are more popular because they are lighter than steel ones, but just as strong: both types have a breaking strain around 2 tonnes (2 tons).

Threaded sleeve

Snap "krabs" have no threaded sleeve on the gate.

• SCREWGATE KARABINER

This has a threaded sleeve that stops the gate from opening by accident. Always use **screwgate karabiners** for main **belays**.

• SNAP KARABINER

These are used mainly for connecting the climbing rope to a **chock** or **sling** to form a **running belay**.

DESCENDEURS

Made from a strong but lightweight alloy, these variable friction devices are used to control the speed of an **abseil** (see pp.70-73). **Descendeurs** connect both to your harness and to the rope. They are also used for **belaying** (see p.47).

• FIGURE OF EIGHT

The most common form of **descendeur**. It is widely available and fairly simple to use.

ANKA •

This offers differing degrees of friction, depending on how the rope is threaded.

BELAY DEVICES

These are friction brakes used to stop the rope from moving during a fall.

TUBER •

This doesn't jam as easily as some other **belay** devices, but requires a little more control when braking (see pp.46-47).

• BELAY PLATE WITH SPRING

This is the original **belay** device. Also called a Sticht Plate, it is straightforward to use. The spring helps keep the rope from jamming.

• BELAY PLATE MINUS SPRING

These need careful rope control in order to prevent jamming. They are highly effective and fairly simple to use.

PACKS & PROTECTION

Packing up, getting a grip, and protecting yourself

ONE MAJOR ADVANCE IN CLIMBING SAFETY over the past 20 years has been the development of **protection** devices to help secure the climbing rope. Placed securely in cracks, they are used as **anchors** or **running belays**. Using them instead of holds (**aid climbing**) is considered unethical by some climbers. Another development is the use of **chalk** to aid grip on handholds.

PACKED FOR ACTION •
Many crags are a long way from the road, so you will need a rucksack in which to carry your **gear** and, perhaps, some food and drink. Avoid those with numerous straps and pockets; the simpler, the better.

• CLIMBERS' "CHALK"
Many climbers carry a small pouch filled with **chalk**. Climbers' chalk – usually sold in blocks – is actually magnesium carbonate powder (the chalk most of us are familiar with is calcium carbonate). Climbers use it to dry sweaty fingers and so improve their grip. The pouch should be lined with fleece material, as this makes it easier to coat your fingers. It should be worn attached to your waist belt, or to the waist belt of your harness.

A POINT OF DEBATE
The use of chalk is controversial; some believe it amounts to "cheating", others deplore it for leaving unsightly marks on the rock.

PROTECTION DEVICES

A wide range of modern **protection** devices is available, which connect to the climbing rope via **slings** or wires and **karabiners**. There are fairly traditional artificial **chockstones**, or **chocks** (a natural chockstone is a rock wedged in a crack), most of which are wedge shaped. Wedge chocks are often called **nuts**. Many chocks are sold on carefully formed wires with high breaking strains. There are also various **camming devices**, which can be securely lodged in awkward positions. Placing devices correctly requires sound judgement, which only comes with experience (see pp.42-43).

• HEXCENTRICS
So-called because they are shaped as "eccentric" (irregular) hexagons, hexcentrics were the first **camming devices**. Available in a wide range of sizes, they are ideal for placing in parallel-sided cracks. The rope holes are drilled so that any strain twists the device more securely into cracks in the rockface (see p.43).

FRIENDS •
Designed to fit into either parallel-sided or slightly flared cracks, these useful devices are usually sold with a tape **sling** already attached.

FLEXIBLE FRIEND •
These hold secure where other devices cannot. The flexible centre wire makes them less prone to leverage than ordinary **friends**.

ROCK ON ROPE •
The original **chocks** were simple wedges. These developed into curved wedges that are known as "rocks".

Tape sling •

ROCK ON WIRE •
High-tensile wire **slings** give greater strength. Wired devices now tend to be the commonest form of **protection**.

• Rope sling

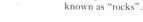
• Wire sling

BANDOLIER •
Although most sit harnesses have **gear** loops, some climbers prefer to carry gear on a bandolier worn around the neck and over one shoulder.

PROTECTION FOR SMALL CRACKS •
Wire **slings** enable smaller devices to be used.

NUT KEY •
A **nut** key aids removal of **protection** devices from stubborn cracks.

Wires are used in small cracks where previously only **pitons** (a type of metal peg) could be used.

THE RIGHT ROPES

Understanding the most basic of climbing tools

YOUR CLIMBING ROPE is the most important piece of safety equipment that you will use, and as such must always be respected accordingly and treated in the correct way. It is not sufficient to use simply any kind of rope – you must make sure that you use one that has been specifically made for climbing. Such ropes are **dynamic** (which means that they stretch slightly when under load) and this helps them to absorb the shock of a fall, which effectively increases the breaking strain. Climbing ropes are sold in two standard lengths: 45m and 50m (150ft and 165ft).

Three strands twisted together

HAWSER-LAID ROPE

Hawser-laid climbing ropes are constructed from 3 separate bunches of continuous nylon filaments that are twisted together. Although perfectly acceptable for novice climbing, this type of rope has been largely superseded by those of **kernmantle** construction.

The kern (core) has many small, hawser-laid cords

Mantle (sheath) of plaited, nylon fibres

KERNMANTLE

Kernmantle ropes consist of a core – or "kern" – of many small, **hawser-laid** cords. This means that each of these cords is made up of twisted nylon filaments. Every one of these filaments runs the full length of the rope. The cords are held together by a tightly plaited sheath called a "mantle". It is this structure that makes **kernmantle** rope so strong, while being extremely flexible and easy to handle.

Each thin, nylon filament runs continuously along the entire length of the rope

THE RANGE OF ROPES

Climbing ropes come in standard lengths of 45m and 50m (150ft and 165ft). They also come in standard thicknesses – numbers 1, 2, 3, and 4 **hawser-laid** ropes being equivalent to 5mm, 7mm, 9mm, and 11mm (¼in, ⅓in, ⅜in, and ½in) **kernmantle** ropes. For a main climbing rope, you need either a number 4 hawser-laid, or an 11mm (½in) kernmantle, rope. Ropes are also used for a number of other purposes, such as **prussik loops** (see p.25) and for threading **chocks** (see pp.42-43). These are normally made from **static rope** (low-stretch). Always use the thickest rope you can, except for prussik loops, which should be made from 5mm (¼in) kernmantle rope.

*5mm (¼in) rope: particularly suitable for **prussik loops** and for threading through small **chocks***

*7mm (⅓in) rope: used principally for threading medium-sized **chocks***

*9mm (⅜in) rope: for threading larger **chocks**, and for some advanced rope techniques*

*11mm (½in) rope: for use as your main climbing rope, for **slings**, and for threading the largest sizes of **chocks***

SIGNS OF ROPE DAMAGE

CORE DAMAGE
Lumps or bulges in rope indicate core damage, even if there is no visible sheath damage. Core-damaged rope is unsafe and should be discarded immediately.

SHEATH DAMAGE
This usually happens when rope rubs across a sharp edge or a rock drops on it. It must be discarded, although undamaged sections can be made into **slings**.

KNOW YOUR KNOTS

Tying the right knot – in the right way – is essential

HAVING CHOSEN THE CORRECT ROPE (see pp.22-23), you must also learn how to choose and tie the correct knot for any given situation. Your interest in knots will develop with climbing experience, but to begin with, limit yourself to the basic ones, and practise until you can, literally, tie them with your eyes closed.

DOUBLE FIGURE OF EIGHT

As this knot is the safest way to form a loop in the main climbing rope, it is often used when **tying on** and when using **anchors**.

1. Form a loop in the double rope, as shown above.

2. Pass the end over the main rope and through the loop.

3. Pull each rope in turn, in order to flatten out the knot.

Figure of eight

THREADED FIGURE OF EIGHT

When you want to tie a loop around something, for example, when tying into a harness (see pp.40-41), you must tie your figure of eight by the threaded method.

1. Form a loose figure of eight in a single strand.

2. Thread the end around the object and back through the knot.

3. Ensure that you follow the path of the single knot exactly.

4. Flatten out the knot and check for unnecessary twists.

PRUSSIK KNOT

This is a slip knot that locks when under load. It is used to tie **prussik loops** onto the main climbing rope (see pp.80-81).

1. Wrap the loop around the main rope.

2. Wrap the loop around the rope again.

3. Pull to tighten.

• *Prussik knot*

DOUBLE FISHERMAN'S KNOT

This is the safest way to make a **sling** (loop) from rope or cord. The 2 knots must be tied in opposite directions.

1. Wrap one end around the rope twice, and through the loops so formed.

2. Pull the knot tight. The end must be at least 10cm (4in) long.

3. Repeat 1-2 with the other end, but form the loops in the opposite direction.

4. Pull both sides of the loop so that the 2 knots fit really snugly together.

• *Double fisherman's knot*

CLOVE HITCH

On popular climbs, previous climbers may have left metal stakes in place at the top to which they **anchored** themselves when **belaying** (see pp.44-49). The safest way to attach to a belay stake is with a tape **sling**, tied in a clove hitch knot.

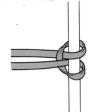

1. Twist the **sling** in such a way that 2 loops are formed, as shown above.

2. Move the top loop over the bottom loop, so that you are trapping the "ends".

3. Place both of the loops over the **belay** stake. Pull the **sling** "ends" tight.

Clove hitch •

APPROACHES TO CLIMBING

The principal ways of tackling a climb

THERE ARE THREE MAIN WAYS to tackle a climb – by **top roping**, **single-pitch**, or **multi-pitch** methods. The method you choose will depend largely on both the nature and height of the rockface, as well as the length of your climbing rope.

TOP ROPING

A good way to climb certain small crags – and an excellent method for beginners

UP AND DOWN

To "top rope", a climber gains the top of the crag by walking around the side (rather than by climbing), **anchors** the climbing rope, and returns to the bottom. Having anchored himself at the foot of the crag, he can now **belay** (control the rope; see pp.44-49) for a climber from below – a good angle from which to observe a novice, and offer advice. Both climber and belayer **tie on** to either end of the rope before the climber sets off. Use this method on crags less than about 20m (65ft) high, where a standard climbing rope easily reaches to the top and back down again.

SAFETY FIRST
The **belayer** at the bottom must be well **anchored**, especially when lighter than the climber: if the latter falls, the belayer could be pulled up the cliff!

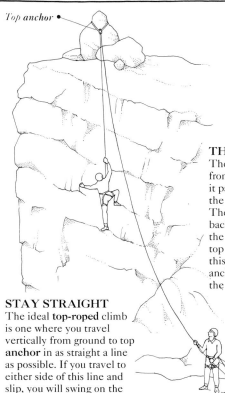

Top anchor •

Tape sling •

Screwgate karabiner •

Climbing rope •

THE PULLEY EFFECT

The climbing rope travels from the ground (that is, from the climber's harness) to the cliff-top, where it passes through a **karabiner** – which must be of the **screwgate** type – attached to a secure **anchor**. The karabiner acts as a pulley. The rope then drops back down to the ground, where it is **belayed** by the climber's partner. If the climber falls, and the top anchor fails, he will hit the ground, so choose this anchor with great care (see pp.42-43). Use 2 anchors if you have any doubts, and ensure that the rope doesn't run over any sharp edges.

STAY STRAIGHT

The ideal **top-roped** climb is one where you travel vertically from ground to top **anchor** in as straight a line as possible. If you travel to either side of this line and slip, you will swing on the rope, and may injure yourself if you hit something.

Bottom anchor •

OTHER APPROACHES

For small crags higher than a rope's length, you can use another **top roping** method: one climber walks to the top, **anchors** himself and **belays** his partner's rope from above (see p.48). Top roping is useful for novices as no one has to **lead** the climb (climb up the rockface first; see pp.28-31 and 76-79).

SAFETY ESSENTIALS

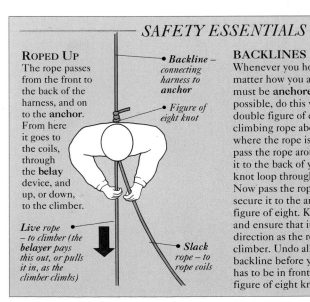

ROPED UP
The rope passes from the front to the back of the harness, and on to the **anchor**. From here it goes to the coils, through the **belay** device, and up, or down, to the climber.

Live rope – to climber (the **belayer** pays this out, or pulls it in, as the climber climbs)

• **Backline** – connecting harness to anchor

• **Figure of eight knot**

• **Slack rope** – to rope coils

BACKLINES
Whenever you hold someone's rope, no matter how you are tackling a climb, you must be **anchored** to the cliff. Where possible, do this with a **backline**. Tie a double figure of eight knot (see p.24) in the climbing rope about 1m (3ft) in front of where the rope is **tied on** to your harness; pass the rope around your side, and connect it to the back of your harness by passing the knot loop through a **screwgate karabiner**. Now pass the rope on to the anchor, and secure it to the anchor with another double figure of eight. Keep your backline tight and ensure that it is running in the same direction as the rope between you and the climber. Undo all the knots forming the backline before you climb. If your anchor has to be in front of you, clip the loop of a figure of eight knot straight into the anchor.

SINGLE-PITCH

*A climb where the route is not suitable for **top roping**,
but can be done easily in one rope length*

IN THE LEAD

PITCH

A **pitch** is the term that is
used to refer to the distance
between consecutive **stances**
(ledges where climbers can
anchor themselves, and **belay**
their climbing partners).

Top roping (see pp.26-27) is
unsuitable where you cannot walk
to the top easily, or if your rope is too
short to reach from the ground to the
top **anchor** and back down again. In
these cases, you will not be able to fix
the top anchor without climbing – and
this means that someone must **lead**.

● KEEPING SAFE
When **belaying** (holding a climber's
rope; see p.44) at the top of a cliff,
ensure that you are **anchored** to the
rock in such a way that you cannot
be pulled over the edge if he falls.

Climbing Sequence

The basics of **single-pitch** climbing are simple. At the base of the cliff, the 2 climbers **tie on** to either end of the rope. One then climbs the cliff, while his rope is held by his partner. When he reaches the top, the climber **anchors** himself (see p.27), then **belays** the rope as his partner climbs.

1. LEADING THE WAY

In most cases, it is the more experienced climber who climbs first. He is called the **leader**, and his partner is the **second**. Having **anchored** himself to the ground, the second ensures that the climbing rope doesn't snag or tangle as the leader climbs.

• *Leader*

• *Second*

2. ANCHORS

As he climbs higher, the **leader** tries to protect himself with **runners**: anchors through which the climbing rope passes (see pp.78-79). For example, if he falls when 2m (6½ft) above a runner, he will only fall about 4m (13ft). Without a good runner, he will almost certainly hit the ground.

• *Runner*

3. AT THE TOP

Once at the top, the **leader anchors** himself securely, then pulls in all the **slack** rope between him and his **second**. He then **belays** his partner, who removes all the **runners** as he climbs. If the second loses his grip, he shouldn't fall far, as the leader is holding the rope.

MULTI-PITCH

How to deal with rockfaces – common in mountainous areas – that are taller than the length of your rope

CLIMBING SEQUENCE

Multi-pitch climbing is often more like serious mountaineering than "rock gymnastics", but the sequence of events is simple. To complete such a climb, one person must **lead**, and the **second** must also be a competent climber. If problems occur, escaping from multi-pitch routes can be tricky – unlike most **single-pitch** climbs, it is impossible to lower a fallen or injured climber to the ground. Good rope management is vital.

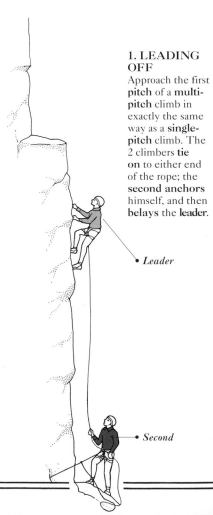

1. LEADING OFF
Approach the first **pitch** of a **multi-pitch** climb in exactly the same way as a **single-pitch** climb. The 2 climbers **tie on** to either end of the rope; the **second anchors** himself, and then **belays** the **leader**.

• *Leader*

• *Second*

EXPOSURE
One major difference between **single-** and **multi-pitch** climbs is the amount of "exposure" – the drop below your feet – that you experience. It is only when you stop at the end of each **pitch**, at the **stance**, that the drop really makes its presence felt. (NOTE: the climbers shown in this photograph are using "double rope" technique, an advanced technique not covered in this book.)

2. THE FIRST STANCE

A short distance before all of the rope has been used up, the **leader** looks for a convenient place to stop (the **stance**) and **anchors** himself safely to the rock. He must then pull in any **slack** rope and **belay** the **second** up the same route. As he climbs, the second removes from the rock any **runners** that the leader has placed.

3. LEADING THROUGH

If the **second** is as experienced as the **leader,** he will often "lead through" – that is, he climbs past the **stance** and leads the next **pitch** himself. If not, he **anchors** himself at the stance, re-sorts the rope (see pp.74-75), and then **belays** the leader as he climbs the next pitch.

ONE PITCH AT A TIME

There are various reasons why a climb may be divided up into several **pitches,** other than the height of the rockface. On difficult or tiring climbs, climbers often welcome a rest at regular intervals. Also, the rock may contain natural ledges, or the route involve many changes in direction, which could cause rope drag (see p.77).

4. CLIMBING ON

This sequence (steps 1-3) continues until the top is reached, the amount of exposure (the drop beneath the climber) increasing with each **pitch**. Finding suitable **stances** with good **anchors** can be a problem, and on many more difficult climbs, you may be forced to **belay** from extremely small ledges.

GRADING SYSTEMS AND GUIDEBOOKS

A look at some of the theory behind the practice

ALTHOUGH YOU CAN MAKE YOUR WAY as you please across a rockface (unless it is on private land or protected for some reason), in most climbing areas there are specific, named routes on each of the major crags. All around the world there are various different grading systems, and routes are graded according to their level of technical difficulty, and perhaps danger – an approximate comparison of some of the more common systems is shown below. These specific routes may also appear in guidebooks, which, like the grading systems, come in all forms – from professionally produced books to photocopied notebooks.

GRADING SYSTEMS

BRITISH SYSTEMS		AMERICAN SYSTEMS		ALPINE (UIAA*)	AUSTRALIAN
Adjectival	Numerical	Yosemite (YDS)	National (NCCS)		
Easy (E)		Class 1	F1	I	1
		Class 2			2
Moderate (Mod)	1a	Class 3	F2	II	3
	1b	Class 4	F3	III-	4
	1c	Class 5.0		III	5
Difficult (Diff)	2a	Class 5.1	F4	III+	6
	2b	Class 5.2		IV-	7
Very Difficult (V Diff)	2c	Class 5.3	F5	IV	8
	3a	Class 5.4		IV+	9, 10
Severe (S)	3b	Class 5.5	F6	V-	11, 12
	4a	Class 5.6		V	13, 14
Very Severe (VS)	4b	Class 5.7	F7	V+	15, 16
	4c	Class 5.8	F8	VI-	17
Hard Very Severe (HVS)	5a				18, 19
	5b	Class 5.9	F9	VI	20
Mild Extremely Severe (E1)		Class 5.10a			21
	5c	Class 5.10b	F10	VII	22
Mild Extremely Severe (E2)		Class 5.10c			23
		Class 5.10d	F11		24
Extremely Severe (E3)	6a	Class 5.11a			25
	6b	Class 5.11b	F12	VIII	26
Extremely Severe (E4)	6c	Class 5.11c			
		Class 5.11d	F13		27
Hard Extremely Severe (E5)	7a	Class 5.12a			
		Class 5.12b			
Hard Extremely Severe (E6)		Class 5.12c		IX	
		Class 5.12d			
Hard Extremely Severe (E7)					

*Union Internationale des Associations d'Alpinisme.

14 Sgurr MhicCoinnich, Coireachan Ruadha Face and Bealach Buttress

MAKING THE GRADE

A specific route is usually given its grade by the first person to climb it. This is why grades should only be viewed as a general guide – no two climbers think exactly alike, and one climber's assessment of climbs in one area may differ from another climber's opinion of routes elsewhere.

NUMERICAL AND ADJECTIVAL

Numerical grades take account of technical difficulty, and are usually based on the hardest move of a climb. Only experience will tell you what is meant by, for example, a "5b" move! Descriptive, or "adjectival", grading also takes account of things like loose rock, exposure, seriousness of a fall, ease of escape, and so on.

GOOD GUIDEBOOKS

A useful guidebook is not simply a list of climbs. Look for those that also provide:

• Background information, such as historical and geological details, rescue facilities, grading system, access, and so on.

• A separate section on each major crag, in which peculiarities about the rock, types of hold, and the ease with which **protection** can be used will be noted.

• Descriptions of the climbs that are detailed enough to allow you to follow the route and avoid any particular dangers.

• Some form of "topo" – diagram – of the route, as shown above.

CLIMBING CALLS

Letting your partner know exactly what you are doing

BECAUSE YOUR SAFETY DEPENDS ultimately on your partner (and vice-versa), each of you must know exactly what the other is doing at any given time. Particularly on **multi-pitch** climbs or large crags, there may be periods when you are out of each other's sight, and so you must have a clear, unambiguous method of communication. This is provided by a series of recognized "climbing calls".

STARTING OUT

Although climbers throughout the world use remarkably similar calls, there are a few differences. It makes sense, therefore, to check with your partner which calls he uses before starting to climb, and agree on a system. Once familiar with the different calls, and the few special constraints, you will find them easy to use and understand.

LEADER •
If the **leader** (the person who climbs the route first; see pp.28-31 and 76-77) falls before he has placed **protection** devices (see pp.42-43), the direction of pull on his partner will be downwards. After he has placed protection, the direction of pull will be up. He must therefore always let his partner know as soon as he has placed the protection, or **runners,** by shouting out clearly: "Runner on!"

WIND NOISE
Shouting at each other may be effective on calm days, but if the wind picks up at all, you will find it difficult – or impossible – to understand what is being said.

Leader •

Second •

SECOND •
As the **leader** climbs, the **second** makes sure the rope pays out freely (see p.47), and shouts when there is only a small amount of rope left, for example: "Five metres!" (sixteen feet). If **protection** nearest the leader falls out, he shouts: "Runner off!"

COMMUNICATION SKILLS

AVOID CONFUSION
If, during the climb, you find you need extra rope, shout "Slack!" Conversely, if you find that there's a lot of **slack** rope and you want it taken in, shout: "Take in!" Never shout "Take in the slack!", because this may lead to confusion. Particularly on a windy day, your partner may only hear "... Slack!" and give you more rope, instead of taking it in.

MULTI-PITCH CLIMBS
The sequence of events, and so of calls, in **multi-pitch** climbing (see pp.30-31) is vital, especially at the start and finish of each **pitch**. The **second** must not let go of the **leader**'s rope until he hears "On belay!" or "Safe!", and must not remove his **anchor** until the leader shouts: "Climb when ready!" If there are other climbers nearby, call each other by name.

FROM THE TOP

It is when the **leader** reaches the top of the **pitch** (stretch between ledges; see pp.28-31) that calls become critical. There is a definite sequence of events, each with its associated call, as detailed here.

LEADER •
When the **leader** hears his partner shout "Slack!" (see box above), he should not immediately pay out a lot of rope, but should allow it to move slowly through his hands, as his partner takes however much is needed.

LEADER AND SECOND
1. The **leader** reaches the top, **anchors** himself, and then shouts: "Safe!"
2. The **second** releases the leader's **belay**, and then prepares to climb.
3. The leader shouts "Taking in!", and pulls in any **slack** rope.
4. When it pulls tight, the second shouts "That's me!"
5. The leader prepares to belay the second, and then shouts: "Climb when ready!"
6. The second removes his anchor and then shouts "Climbing!", but waits for the leader to acknowledge with an "Okay!" before he starts.

SECOND •
If the **second** becomes nervous, he should shout: "Tight rope!" This lets his partner know that he needs assistance. Before a fall, there is usually a period when the climber is fighting to stay "in contact" (with the rock), so it's usually possible to call out a warning.

LOOSE ROCK
If a rock becomes dislodged at any time during a climb, bellow: "Below!"

THE WEEKEND COURSE

Your ready-reference plan of action for the two-day course

THE COURSE COVERS 12 SKILLS, divided into two days of practice. Your first day begins with easy-to-follow steps to safe rope management, **tying on** and **anchoring** yourself. Day 1 continues with controlling your climbing partner's rope, useful handholds and footholds to look for, and a series of basic rock climbing moves. On Day 2, you will learn some more advanced holds, as well as the specific moves needed to tackle different rockface features – and how to get out of certain tricky situations. Place what you learn against the background of the Mountain Code, and think about improving your technique and finding exciting places to climb (see pp.84-91).

Tuber belaying device

DAY 1		Hours	Page
SKILL 1	Learning the ropes	½	38-39
SKILL 2	Tying on	½	40-41
SKILL 3	Fixing anchors	½	42-43
SKILL 4	Belaying	1½	44-49
SKILL 5	Using basic holds	1	50-51
SKILL 6	First moves	2	52-57

Anchoring *the climb*

Effective rope management

KEY TO SYMBOLS

CLOCKS
Small clocks appear on the first page of each new skill. The blue section shows how long you might spend on that skill, and where that skill fits into your day. For example, check the clock on p.40. The blue segment shows that ½ hour should be set aside for Skill 2 (which is "Tying on"), and the grey segment shows that ½ hour was spent on the previous skill. But be flexible, use clocks as a guideline only, and settle in to a natural pace.

RATING SYSTEM ••••
Each skill is given a rating according to the degree of difficulty. One bullet (•) denotes that the skill is comparatively straightforward, while five bullets (•••••) are given to the most challenging skills.

MICRO-MEN
The series of micro-men, next to each skill step, shows the number of steps in that skill. Blue men identify the step that is being illustrated.

ARROWS
Blue arrows (left) show a direction of movement or pressure. However, on pp.44-47, they are used more specifically: the solid arrows show that the hand grips the rope so that the hand and the rope move in the same direction. Arrows with a broken line (right) show that the hand slides along the rope in that direction, but the rope stays still.

DAY 2		Hours	Page
SKILL 7	Moving on	½	58-59
SKILL 8	Overcoming obstacles	2	60-69
SKILL 9	Abseiling	1	70-73
SKILL 10	Multi-pitch climbing	½	74-75
SKILL 11	Taking the lead	1	76-79
SKILL 12	Self-help	1	80-83

Different handholds for different situations

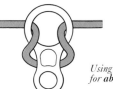

*Using devices for **abseiling***

Using your boot sole for maximum grip

1

LEARNING THE ROPES

Definition: *Looking after your most vital piece of safety equipment*

YOUR MOST VITAL ALLY where climbing safety is concerned is your climbing rope. Looked after and used properly, it will perform well – and may save your life. Treated badly, it could kink and tangle at the most awkward times, and could even precipitate an accident. Fortunately, the basics of correct rope management are easy to grasp.

OBJECTIVE: To make your rope run freely, without tangling. *Rating* •

UNCOILING ROPE

One of the first things you have to do at the base of a climb is uncoil your rope. The exact method used depends on how you coiled it (see p.39), but the end result is the same – you should undo the binding, then uncoil it carefully, loop by loop, letting each loop fall to the ground to form a pile of loose coils. Never throw it on the ground or climb until you have run it through your hands at least once.

SAFETY FIRST •
Get into the habit of feeling the rope every time you run it through your hands. Check it carefully for abrasion, swellings, or other distortions (see pp.22-23), and discard any suspect rope. Never tread on your rope – there may be a sharp stone underneath!

GENERAL CARE
Store your rope lightly coiled in a dark, airy cupboard, well away from sources of heat and sunlight. Only use it for climbing – never use it as a tow rope, as this will seriously weaken it.

MOUNTAINEER'S COILS

Rope should be coiled for easy storage and carrying. For "Mountaineer's Coiling", form a series of loops stretching from just above your waist to just below your knee.

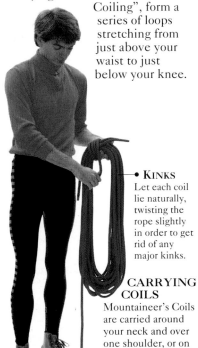

• **KINKS**
Let each coil lie naturally, twisting the rope slightly in order to get rid of any major kinks.

CARRYING COILS
Mountaineer's Coils are carried around your neck and over one shoulder, or on your back like a rucksack (see under "Alpine Coils").

ALPINE COILS

With "Alpine (or Butterfly) Coiling", start from the middle of the rope, then form a series of loops, each one a full arm span's length, putting each loop around your neck as you go.

WEARING THE COIL
Remove the coils from around your neck and bind together as shown in the box below. To wear the coil on your back, separate the 2 rope ends, pass them over your shoulders and tie them together round your waist.

FINISHING OFF THE COIL

MOUNTAINEER'S
1. Pass the end you started with back over itself to form a loop. Wind the other end around the coils a few times. 2. Pass the end through the loop. Pull the loop end firmly to secure.

ALPINE
Wrap some rope around the coils; pass a loop through the "hole"; pass the ends through the loop.

1

2

SKILL

DAY 1

2 TYING ON

Definition: *Connecting the rope securely to your harness*

IT IS NOT ENOUGH SIMPLY TO BUY a good harness and safety rope – you must be able to connect the two securely. Although basic techniques are similar, there are no rigid rules, and different harnesses require you to **tie on** in slightly different ways. Only buy a harness that comes with instructions on attaching the main rope. With practice, you should be able to tie on blindfold!

OBJECTIVE: To create the safest climber-to-rope unit.
Rating • •

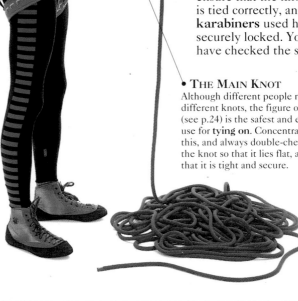

SAFETY CHECKS

Once **tied on**, you should go through a series of safety checks. In particular, ensure that the knot securing the rope is tied correctly, and check that all **karabiners** used have the **screwgate** securely locked. You should already have checked the state of your rope.

• THE MAIN KNOT

Although different people recommend different knots, the figure of eight knot (see p.24) is the safest and easiest one to use for **tying on**. Concentrate as you tie this, and always double-check it. "Dress" the knot so that it lies flat, and ensure that it is tight and secure.

BEFORE YOU CLIMB

Once **tied on** and ready to go, check that you're wearing your helmet, and that your boot laces are tied. Such things are easy to forget!

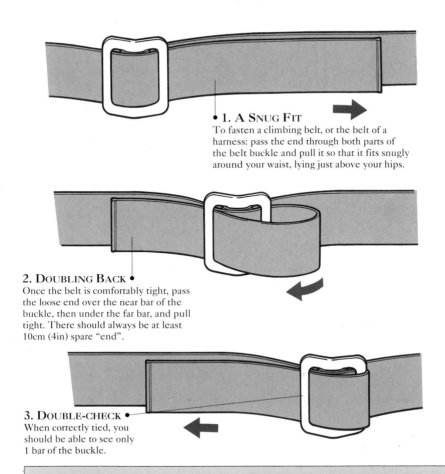

• 1. A SNUG FIT
To fasten a climbing belt, or the belt of a
harness: pass the end through both parts of
the belt buckle and pull it so that it fits snugly
around your waist, lying just above your hips.

2. DOUBLING BACK •
Once the belt is comfortably tight, pass
the loose end over the near bar of the
buckle, then under the far bar, and pull
tight. There should always be at least
10cm (4in) spare "end".

3. DOUBLE-CHECK •
When correctly tied, you
should be able to see only
1 bar of the buckle.

KNOW YOUR ROPE – AND YOUR ROCKFACE

WHICH END IS WHICH?
When you form a pile of coils, you cause
the rope to have a "top" and a "bottom"
end. The bottom end is the end you
started with, and so is at the bottom of the
pile of coils; the top end is the end you
finished with, and is at the top of the pile.
If you pull the bottom end, the rope comes
from beneath the coils, loops get caught
around loops, and a tangle (known as
"knitting") quickly forms – which can
cause problems. If you pull the top end,
the rope should pay out freely. The **leader**
of a climb (see pp.76-77) must therefore
always **tie on** to the top end of the rope,
and the **second** on the bottom end.

THE RIGHT ATTITUDE
To succeed at climbing, you must want to
climb – there is no point in climbing
unless you enjoy it. Although different
people climb in different ways, a calm,
considered approach is generally more
successful than an aggressive one.
Climbing should start from the moment
you first see the rockface. As you approach,
look at the rock and get a feel for its shape,
structure, and major features. While **tying
on**, look at the route you are about to
climb and visualize various moves,
particularly sections that appear difficult.
You should climb as much with your head
as with your hands and feet.

3 FIXING ANCHORS

Definition: *Using devices to secure your climb*

YOU NEED ANCHORS to secure yourself to the cliff when **belaying**, and for **protection** (see pp.76-79). They must be totally reliable. While the most natural anchor – placing a **sling** around a tree or small pinnacle of rock – is highly effective, special devices are also used, as shown here, and modern designs make fixing anchors far easier than it used to be. Devices are fastened to a sling, which is linked to the climbing rope by a **karabiner**. Placing anchors requires practice and should be demonstrated by an experienced climber.

OBJECTIVE: Learning the correct location for the right type of **anchor**.
Rating • •

A CLIMBER'S FRIEND
Above: A **friend** is a **camming device** that is used to form an effective **anchor** in parallel-sided, or even slightly flared, cracks. The original style of friend has 4 cams; more recent designs have 3 (see p.21).

THREADS
Left: You can sometimes "thread" a tape **sling** behind a natural **chockstone** or through a "hole" in the rock, forming an **anchor** that resists pull from any direction.

FROM A HEX TO A FRIEND

HEXCENTRICS

Hexcentrics, or hexes (right), are "eccentric" (irregular) alloy hexagons with a rope **sling** threaded through in such a way that any pull creates a **camming** effect, twisting the hexcentric more securely against the sides of the crack in which it is placed. They are available in various sizes, to fit large or small cracks (see p.21).

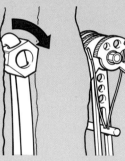

BEST FRIENDS

Friends (left) allow highly secure **anchors** to be placed in climbs that were previously thought to be "unprotectable". However, they are expensive, so don't place them deep inside cracks where they are difficult to retrieve. Ensure that the "stem" can't act like a lever and weaken the anchor.

LARGE HEX

Place a hex in a crack so that it **cams** tighter when under load (see box above). It can also be placed lengthways, like a wedge.

WEDGE

This tapering piece of metal alloy on a **sling** is placed in a crack above a narrowing to form an artificial **chockstone**.

ROCKS

These are simply curved wedges. Working on the same principle as wedges, they are usually more secure and often easier to place.

WIRES

Smaller rocks are often sold with strong wire **slings**. Use with an added "extension" sling to prevent displacement (see pp.78-79).

SKILL

DAY 1

4 BELAYING

Definition: *Holding the climbing rope in such a way that you reduce the risk of a partner's slip becoming a fall*

BELAYING – THE BASICS OF WHICH you must master – is a way of holding the rope for a partner (once you are **tied on** and **anchored**; see pp.40 & 27) so that you have the best chance of preventing him from hitting the ground if he falls. It is also an easy and efficient way of paying out and taking in rope with little risk of knots, kinks, and tangles.

OBJECTIVE: To hold the climbing rope in order to pay out, take in, and hold a fall with a minimum of effort. *Rating* ● ● ●

BODY BELAY

Belaying without equipment, using the friction of the rope around the body

TAKING IN LIVE ROPE

Pass the rope over your shoulders, letting it drop down around your waist. Identify the **live** rope (L, the part of the rope that goes to the climber) and the **slack** rope (S, the part that goes to the pile of coils). Twist the slack rope around the outside of your forearm.
(The "live hand" is the hand that starts out next to the live rope, the "slack hand" next to the slack rope.)

— Step 1 —
STARTING OFF

With your elbows held in at your sides, and your hands at waist height, hold the **live** rope and the **slack** rope in your live hand, immediately forward of your slack hand.

— Step 2 —
SLIDE BACK

Hold both ropes firmly with your **live** hand. Slide your **slack** hand back along the rope until it is just forward of your waist.

Solid arrows=hand and rope movement. Broken arrows=hand movement only.

— Step 3 —
PULL IN

Grip with your **slack** hand and move it forward. Pull in the rope, letting the **live** and slack ropes slide through your live hand.

PAYING OUT LIVE ROPE

This is virtually the reverse of taking in. However, you must keep the twist in the **slack** rope. If you mistakenly take a twist in the **live** rope, and your partner falls, he may break your arm.

START OFF

With elbows at sides and hands at waist height, hold the **live** and **slack** ropes in your slack hand, just forward of your live hand.

DRAW BACK

Holding both ropes firmly with your **slack** hand, slide your **live** hand back along the rope until it is just forward of your waist.

FEED THROUGH

Grip with your **live** hand and move it forward, thus paying out the rope. To make this easier, turn the palm of your **slack** hand towards your body.

HOLDING A FALL

YOUR BODY TAKES THE STRAIN

As soon as your partner slips, or even before, hold on tight to the rope with your **slack** hand, and move your slack forearm across your chest. The strain will be taken by the amount of friction around your body. To do this efficiently, never over-reach when **belaying**. Always feed the rope from one hand to the other so that you don't have to reach forward or down to pick up a dropped rope. Wear gloves and long sleeves when using body belays, to prevent the possibility of getting rope burns on your hands or arms.

MODERN METHODS

SKILL
4

*Belaying techniques that use specially designed friction brakes
rather than wrapping the rope around your body*

SLACK AND LIVE

You must note which is the **slack** (S), and which the **live** (L), rope.

BELAY PLATES

The most widely used piece of modern **belaying** equipment is the "belay plate" (see p.19). The various models all work on the same principle: the nearer the plate is to the harness **karabiner**, the greater the friction, and so the better the "stopping power".

——— Step 1 ———
SETTING IT UP

Connect a **screwgate karabiner** to the front attachment point of your harness, with the gate uppermost and opening away from you. Pass a loop of climbing rope through one of the slots on the **belay** plate; clip this loop into the karabiner, with the **slack** rope uppermost, and do up the gate.

S

L

BRAKING
To lock the device and hold a fall, pull the **live** rope up and back.

LOCK OFF
When not actively moving the rope, lock off the **belay** plate by separating the ropes as much as possible.

SLOTS & SPRINGS
If the 2 slots on the **belay** plate are different sizes, use the larger one. The spring, if present, should be nearest the **karabiner**.

L   S

BELAYING POINTERS

PRECISION DEVICES

In addition to a wide number of **belay** plates, you can also belay using **descendeurs** such as the "figure of eight" (see p.19) and tubular devices (tubers) such as the one shown here. Although these tubular models are extremely efficient, they require a degree of precision, and many novices find that they tend to jam easily.

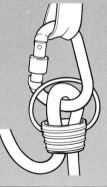

USE AND MISUSE

Modern **belaying** equipment must only ever be used with **kernmantle** rope. Although modern devices are relatively easy to use, many climbers do not pay enough attention to their grip on the **slack** (braking) side of the device. In order to brake quickly and effectively, you must ensure that you have hold of the slack rope at all times.

Step 2

ON THE SLIDE

When using a **belay** plate, think of it as a sliding brake, and the **karabiner** as a pulley. The nearer the plate to the karabiner, the greater the braking power. The closer the **slack** rope to the **live** rope, the easier it is to take in or pay out. To take in the live rope, slide your hands along the rope as shown. Don't let go of either side.

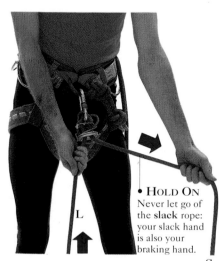

• HOLD ON
Never let go of the **slack** rope: your slack hand is also your braking hand.

BRAKING POWER
The greater the angle between the ropes as they enter the plate, the greater the braking power.

Step 3

MOVING IT THROUGH

When your **live** hand gets near the **karabiner**, let go of the live rope and grasp the **slack** rope just beyond your slack hand. Slide your slack hand to the karabiner, replace your live hand on the live rope, and repeat step 2. Paying out the live rope is simpler: just slide your hands along the rope (see step 2). Don't let go of either side.

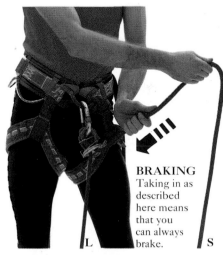

BRAKING
Taking in as described here means that you can always brake.

JAMMING
If the rope jams, bring both ropes close together, moving the **belay** plate away from the **karabiner** with the **live** hand. Don't release the **slack** rope.

TOP BELAY

An "indirect" belay – taking the climber's weight – from above

• **Backline**
*(securing
belayer to
anchor)*

—— FROM THE TOP ——

SAFETY CHECKLIST
When you are **belaying** someone from above, there are various factors that you should consider, especially the danger of being pulled off if your partner falls.

• Ensure that your **anchor** is "bombproof" (reliable), even if this means **tying on** to 2 or more points. It should be above you – to resist downward pull.

• Keep the **backline** (see p.27), connecting you to your anchor, tight, to stop you being pulled over the edge.

• Stand so that the backline runs in the same direction as the force of your partner's possible fall – so that you are not pulled sideways.

• **STANCE**
Stand with a firm, braced posture, tight on your **backline**, and in a position where you can see as much of your partner as possible.

INDIRECT BELAYING
The **belay** shown here is "indirect": that is, as with the body belay (see pp.44-45), the belayer's body takes much of the climber's weight.

TENSION
Ensure that there is a minimum of **slack** in the system. Keep the rope tight without causing discomfort or actually helping your partner to climb.

CONCENTRATION
Concentrate on your partner. A good **belayer** senses when a climber is in difficulty simply by watching their climbing posture and the way that they move.

DIRECT BELAY

Using an anchor to take the climber's weight

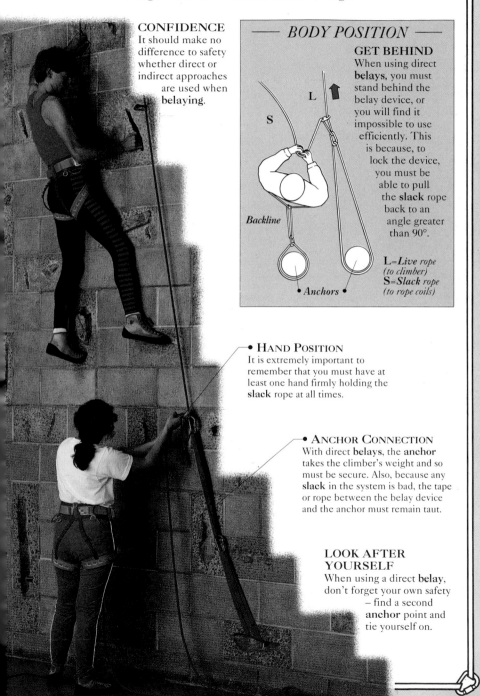

CONFIDENCE
It should make no difference to safety whether direct or indirect approaches are used when **belaying.**

BODY POSITION

GET BEHIND
When using direct **belays,** you must stand behind the belay device, or you will find it impossible to use efficiently. This is because, to lock the device, you must be able to pull the **slack** rope back to an angle greater than 90°.

Backline

L=*Live rope (to climber)*
S=*Slack rope (to rope coils)*

• *Anchors* •

• **HAND POSITION**
It is extremely important to remember that you must have at least one hand firmly holding the **slack** rope at all times.

• **ANCHOR CONNECTION**
With direct **belays,** the **anchor** takes the climber's weight and so must be secure. Also, because any **slack** in the system is bad, the tape or rope between the belay device and the anchor must remain taut.

LOOK AFTER YOURSELF
When using a direct **belay,** don't forget your own safety – find a second **anchor** point and tie yourself on.

5 USING BASIC HOLDS

Definition: *Techniques to adopt for the more obvious kinds of hold*

ALTHOUGH MANY ROCK CLIMBING MOVES are instinctive, there are certain techniques you can use to make good holds better, and all kinds of hold safer. Here we are primarily concerned with obvious holds; later on (see pp.58-59), you will be introduced to less distinct holds. To be of use, a hold must be firm and within convenient reach. If you think it is loose, test it with a kick, or a blow from the heel of your hand. Although you should avoid loose holds whenever possible, they are often secure enough to be used in one direction, but not another. No matter what the hold, avoid using your knees (see pp.52-53).

OBJECTIVE: To make the most of obvious holds. *Rating* • •

HANDHOLDS

Handholds should usually be used to maintain balance, not for pulling yourself up the cliff. This means that handholds don't have to be large.

SMALL "PEBBLE"
This can be used to steady yourself as you move. If above you, pinch it between thumb and forefinger (as shown); if below, cover it with the heel of your hand and push down.

LARGE PINCH-GRIP
Larger pebbles or flakes of rock can be held in the same way as you would hold a brick. Grip as hard as you can, as if trying to make your fingers pass through the rock and meet. The rougher the rock, the better the friction.

MEDIUM "JUG"
"Jugs" are holds around which you can curve your hand – grab hold and feel safe. On easy climbs they may be massive; on harder ones they may be finger-sized, or totally absent.

SIDE PULLS
Don't just use handholds above you. You will often find holds on either side which are adequate to hold you in balance. If you can also use your thumb – so much the better.

FOOTHOLDS

Because you should climb with your legs rather than your arms, footholds are extremely important.

EDGING
Rather than strain your calf muscles on small toe-holds, it is much better to **edge** – use the inside of your foot.

MEDIUM BLOCK
Unless you can place all your boot sole on the hold, keep heels low. Never stand on tiptoe to reach a higher hold.

• UNDERCUTS
By keeping hands low, you can often make good use of undercut (upside-down) holds.

LARGE "POCKET"
Footholds needn't stick out. With big pockets, watch your balance, and don't strain your arms.

PLANS
Working out the best combination of holds to make a move is highly satisfying.

6

FIRST MOVES

Definition: *Moving from hold to hold to progress over the rock*

ANY ONE CLIMB MAY INVOLVE a range of different moves. To find a safe route up the rockface you may well move upwards, downwards, and sideways. It is making these moves effectively that forms the first principles of good rock climbing. Remember that, unless you are climbing at very low levels, you should always be attached to a rope.

OBJECTIVE: To move smoothly, steadily, and safely from hold to hold, using the minimum amount of energy. *Rating* ● ● ●

LOW-LEVEL TRAVERSING

Moving sideways along the base of the cliff, a short distance above the ground – an ideal way to practise climbing

—————— Step 1 ——————

WORKING IT OUT

Climb with your eyes and brain as well as your arms and legs. Work out where you want to go before moving: not just the general route, but also the precise holds.

STABILITY ●———————
Plan several moves at a time from a position where you feel safe. Spreading arms and legs wide may increase stability.

THE RIGHT COMBINATIONS
Try to work out combinations of handholds and footholds that, when brought together in a particular sequence, will enable you to move smoothly across the rock with the least effort.

PUTTING IN PRACTICE
Difficult **traversing** moves can be practised on any available rock – even the most insignificant boulders.

FEEL THE ROCK
Run your fingers over the rock to find less obvious holds.

Step 2
MAKING THE MOVE

Move from one position to the next smoothly and purposefully. If you can't do it, return to your original position and replan.

EXPERIMENT
Don't be afraid to experiment when **traversing**. Everyone climbs differently – develop a style that you find comfortable.

• LOOK OUT
Guide your hands and feet to each hold with your eyes. On steep rock, you may have to lean back slightly to see footholds.

• POSTURE
Don't lean into the rock or raise your hands too high. Stand up straight, with your body weight over your feet.

• ACCURACY
Particularly when using smaller holds, place your hands and feet carefully and precisely. Guide them to the correct position with your eyes. Don't flail around in the hope that you might come across a suitable hold – you won't!

ASCENDING

Moving yourself upwards on the rockface

----- Step 1 -----
PLANNING AHEAD

Look around and decide where your hands and feet will move to. Plan several moves ahead. Do this throughout your climb; it is especially important for ascending.

EYES
Look all around, not just up. There may be good holds to either side or below.

HAND HEIGHT
You'll get better balance if you keep your hands around shoulder height.

----- Step 2 -----
GOING UP

Propel yourself up to this higher position, where you gain new holds, by pushing down on the footholds and straightening the legs.

HOLD ON
Use handholds for balance only. Don't pull yourself up with your hands.

CONTACT
Keep 3 points of contact with the rock: 1 hand and both feet or both hands and 1 foot. This means that you should only be moving 1 limb at a time.

DON'T DITHER
Move deliberately and smoothly. If moves won't work, go back to your previous hold(s).

A GOOD GRIP •
Handholds need not be directly above you. In fact, these are often the least suitable, especially if they are close to your body. Using holds to either side provides a stable base, and makes further movement easier.

SPACING HOLDS
Use holds that you can reach comfortably. One long step may use more energy than 2 or 3 smaller steps and, especially on a long climb, you must learn to conserve your strength. Use small, intermediate holds whenever possible.

BALANCE
The secret of safe ascending is smooth and steady progress, using the least amount of energy necessary to make each move. Place your body in a balanced, comfortable position. Avoid cramped or strained positions – these will only tire you more rapidly.

LEG •
Your leg muscles are the most powerful muscles in your body. Ascending uses these muscles more than any others to push your body up the rockface.

—————————— Step 3 ——————————

MOVING ON

To continue ascending, propel yourself upwards by pushing right down on the footholds and straightening your legs.
Use your hands to stay in balance. Think of climbing stairs; you don't pull yourself up using the step above; you place your foot deliberately on each step and push up with your legs.

DESCENDING

How to move down a section of rock

EYES
Look all around for possible holds.

• HANDS
Get your hands as low as possible before moving your feet.

A VITAL SKILL
Too often neglected, descending is an important skill that can be useful for getting out of awkward situations.

FOOT NOTE •
Don't scrabble around, hoping your foot will find a hold. Look for holds, and place your feet deliberately.

--------------- Step 1 ---------------

LOOKING AROUND

Look around and plan your moves in advance. Move your hands down before your feet. Descending can be awkward because the holds are not as easy to see as they are when ascending.

• FOOTHOLDS
As your leg moves down and you place your foot on a hold, remember to keep your heel low: standing on "tiptoe" makes your feet far less secure.

• STEP-BY-STEP
Don't move your feet too far down in one go.

Step 2
MOVING DOWN

As you lower your feet to move down, your arms straighten and your hands are left above head height. Find lower alternatives for handholds.

LOOK OUT
Look around all the time, and don't be afraid to change route: holds that were hidden may reappear, or holds that previously looked good may suddenly seem less attractive!

• HANDHOLDS
By using handholds to either side of the line of descent, you will find that you have a stable posture from which to lean out slightly in order to see holds.

EYES •
Use your eyes to guide your feet to the holds. Concentrate and use precise movements.

ANGLED ROCK
On gently angled rock, descend facing outwards. Keep hands low and rest on your buttocks while planning moves. As the angle steepens, turn side on, finally facing inwards as the rock becomes vertical.

Step 3
STAYING STEADY

Move down 1 hold at a time. Use your leg muscles to lower yourself and your arms for balance. Keep your weight over your feet.

PRACTICE
You will find that descending feels unnatural and requires a fair amount of practice before it can be achieved with confidence. Don't let this stop you from trying. It is a useful technique on any crag, but should be regarded as essential by anyone visiting big mountain- or cliff-faces.

IN CONTROL
Never drop onto a hold – it may not be as good as it looks, and you may not be able to climb back up if further descent proves impossible.

• SMEARS
Smearing footholds rely on keeping as much boot sole in contact with the rock as possible. Keep your heels low.

SKILL

7

MOVING ON

Definition: *Ways of using less obvious holds*

DAY 2

SOONER OR LATER you will come across rock that offers few holds. If there are handholds but not footholds, you can progress by **smearing** your feet against the rock in order to get maximum friction. If there are footholds but no handholds, try progressing by selecting a route that allows you to stay in balance. If there are cracks, you may be able to **jam.**

OBJECTIVE: Making the best use of less distinct holds. *Rating* • • •

HANDHOLDS

Handholds needn't stick out to be of use. You can often progress by using "pockets" and "**jam**-cracks".

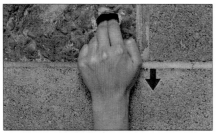

SMALL POCKETS
Insert 1 or 2 fingers as far as possible, placing your palm flat against the rock.

"FINGER LOCK": SMALL CRACKS
Insert 2 fingers just above a narrowing in the crack, twist your wrist, and pull down.

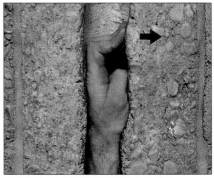

HAND JAM: WIDE CRACKS
Insert the hand above a narrower part; push with the fingers; bend your thumb across your palm.

OTHER JAMS
There are as many types of **jam** as there are sizes of crack. The one shown here is small, but for massive cracks, jam part of your body – for example all of your arm – across the gap, just above a place where it narrows further.

FOOTHOLDS

Used correctly, minute irregularities
will hold your weight. In addition to
using **smearing** (friction) footholds,
you can also **jam** with your feet.

EDGING
Unless **smearing**, use the inside of your foot
on tiny edges. Place feet with great care.

FOOT JAM
The simplest kind of foot **jam** is where you
simply place your foot in a crack, preferably
just above a narrowing of the crack.
Remember that you must keep your heel
low, especially where the crack is so small
that it will only admit your toes.

PRECISION
The smaller the hold, the more carefully you
must place your foot. Once in position, keep
it absolutely still to avoid slipping.

JAMMING

HAND JAM

1. Place your hand
in the crack, just
above a narrowing.
It may be more
effective with your thumb
towards the bottom.

2. Push the back
of your hand
against one side,
your fingertips
against the other, and bring
your thumb across your palm.

3. Twist slightly with your
wrist and pull. Your
hand shouldn't
move – if it does,
it will hurt!

FOOT JAM

1. Twist your foot
sideways and push
it into the crack,
preferably above
a narrowing.

2. Twist your foot
back as level as it
will go, so that each
side is trapped in
the crack.

3. Lower your heel
to complete the
jam. Remember –
you must untwist
your foot before you
can remove it!

SKILL

8 OVERCOMING OBSTACLES

DAY 2

Definition: *Techniques for tackling common rockface features*

ONE OF THE MAJOR CLIMBING SKILLS is being able to overcome the obstacles that can bar access to the next section of crag. Although making progress is often simply a matter of working out the correct combination or sequence of handholds and footholds, certain obstacles can only be overcome by employing specific techniques.

OBJECTIVE: To match the correct move to a specific obstacle. *Rating* • • • •

LAYBACKING

A useful method of ascending an offset face of rock

PUSH AND PULL
Your legs push against the rock while your arms pull against the rock edge.

• **EYES UP**
Keep your eyes on the next handhold.

LAYAWAY
Above: A **layaway** is a **layback** used for a single move. Move quickly and deliberately.

—— Step 1 ——
LEAN BACK

Start off in the classic **layback** position: leaning back and gripping the edge of the rock with your hands.

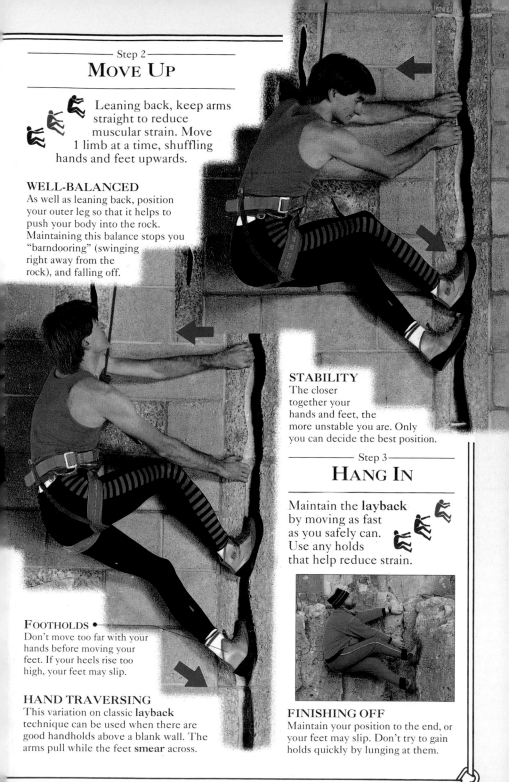

MOVE UP

Leaning back, keep arms straight to reduce muscular strain. Move 1 limb at a time, shuffling hands and feet upwards.

WELL-BALANCED

As well as leaning back, position your outer leg so that it helps to push your body into the rock. Maintaining this balance stops you "barndooring" (swinging right away from the rock), and falling off.

STABILITY

The closer together your hands and feet, the more unstable you are. Only you can decide the best position.

HANG IN

Maintain the **layback** by moving as fast as you safely can. Use any holds that help reduce strain.

FOOTHOLDS •

Don't move too far with your hands before moving your feet. If your heels rise too high, your feet may slip.

HAND TRAVERSING

This variation on classic **layback** technique can be used when there are good handholds above a blank wall. The arms pull while the feet **smear** across.

FINISHING OFF

Maintain your position to the end, or your feet may slip. Don't try to gain holds quickly by lunging at them.

SKILL

BRIDGING

Spreading the body between holds to **bridge** *a gap*

Step 1
GETTING A HOLD

As you approach a gap, start looking for handholds and footholds on either side of that gap.

SAVE YOUR STRENGTH
Unlike **laybacking** (see pp.60-61), **bridging** moves need not be too strenuous.

STABILITY
Keeping your arms and legs apart whenever possible gives you greater stability.

Step 2
START THE SPAN

Move into the holds and so into the **bridging** position.

BALANCE
You may have to move quite quickly to gain the **bridge**.

• **FOOTHOLDS**
Many **bridging** footholds are sloping; some rely on friction. Try to keep heels low and as much of your sole in contact with the rock as possible.

MOVING UP
Try using opposing pressures to ascend a gap. For example, push with your left hand and right foot, while moving your left foot up and keeping balance with your right hand.

STRETCH
Do regular stretching exercises – suppleness is essential for climbing.

AT REST
Once established, you will find the **bridge** surprisingly stable. On strenuous climbs, it is often used as a way of resting, as little muscular effort is needed to maintain the position.

EXPOSED
Bridging can put you into an exposed position, which may be unnerving to start with.

HANDS •
To conserve strength, keep your hands at shoulder height or below when you are resting.

Step 3

THE BRIDGE

• SURE FEET
While getting established in the span, make a conscious effort to push your feet into the holds.

Having gained the **bridge**, keep yourself in the position by simply pushing outwards in opposite directions with your legs.

BRIDGING DIFFERENT GAPS
As well as offering a means of rest during strenuous climbs, **bridging** can be used in wide **chimneys**, and in open corners with virtually blank walls. It can also be useful for passing overhanging rock, because by bridging below the **overhang**, it is often possible to gain its lip and conquer it with little effort (see pp.68-69).

CORNER CLIMBING
To use **bridging** for climbing corners: With 1 foot and 1 hand each side of the corner, push in opposite directions.

MANTELLING

*A method of gaining a ledge or another form of foothold
by using only that hold*

Step 1

THE APPROACH

Approach the ledge in
such a way that you can
hold it firmly with both
hands, then start to run your
feet up the wall below.

• MAKING ROOM
It is important to lean back slightly on
your hands – to see what you are doing
and to give your feet space to move.

WRISTS •
When you grip with your hands,
keep your wrists flexible. This
is because, as you gain height,
you will need to change from a
pull grip to a push.

OUT OF REACH
You will find that **mantelling**
is particularly useful when you
want to get to good holds that
are initially out of reach because
they are situated above a ledge.

OVERHANGS
Where the ledge juts out from the
main face, it forms an **overhang**
or bulge (see pp.10-11). Tackling
this strains the arm muscles, so
it is important to **mantel** both
quickly and smoothly.

USING DOWN-PRESSURE
Mantelling moves can be adapted
to all kinds of situations.

FOOTHOLDS •
Use small holds to
gain height quickly
and lessen the strain
on your arms.

HEAD •
With practice, you will get a feel for how your head position affects your balance, and so, in turn, affects the strain on your arms.

OBSERVATION •
Look around for your next handhold – but keep your head close to the rock to maintain balance.

BALANCE •
Small footholds aid balance and reduce arm strain.

• **CHANGING OVER**
The critical part is changing your handgrip from a pull to a push. Get 1 foot fairly high and use small holds or **smears** to reduce strain on your wrists during this changeover.

─── Step 2 ───
FROM PULL TO PUSH

Move your feet up, then change your handgrip from an upward pull to a downward push. If you tire, you may find that you are able to rest on your forearms at this stage.

─── Step 3 ───
ONTO THE LEDGE

Push down with your hands and straighten your arms, then raise 1 foot up onto the ledge. Balance is vital at this stage; using small footholds helps. Hold yourself in position while you find a higher handhold, then stand on the ledge. Do all 3 steps in one smooth and continuous movement.

CHIMNEYING

A method of climbing cracks that are wide enough to admit the whole body

───── Step 1 ─────
INTO THE GAP

In wide cracks (shown here), brace your legs across the gap and push out with your hands and feet. In narrow slits, place your hands and knees on one side, your feet and back on the other.

CHECK IT OUT
Before entering the **chimney**, have a good look at what is to come, and decide which way you are going to face. Although you may be able to turn around, it can often be a tricky manoeuvre.

HOW FAR IN?
It is often better to stay near the edge of the **chimney**, where you can use holds on the outside face, rather than squirming deep inside the crack, where the rock may be damp and slippery.

HANDS •
The most useful handhold is the pressure hold. Keep your fingers pointing down.

───── *MAKING THE BEST PROGRESS* ─────

CHOCKSTONES
In some **chimneys**, you may find your upward progress hampered by a natural **chockstone**. You will have to decide whether to pass it on the inside (if there is room), or on the outside. It is easier to move into the correct orientation earlier rather than later – if you climb directly underneath the chockstone, it will hide much of the route above. When passing chockstones, no matter how large or small, treat them with respect. Although those on popular routes are probably fairly solid, some are not above suspicion!

BRIDGING
In wide **chimneys**, you may find that **bridging** is the best method of ascent (see pp.62-63). When the holds are reasonable, climb in the usual way, moving each arm and leg alternately. When there are few holds, progress is possible by using friction. In this method, it is better to keep hands low, with your fingers pointing down, pushing as much of the palm and heel of your hand as possible against each wall, in order to gain maximum friction. In this method, hold your position with both hands while moving both feet up.

Step 3
MOVING UP

Having braced 1 foot on the "back" wall as a second step, brace a hand on the wall in front, and move up by taking your buttocks and back off the rock and replacing them higher up.

HANDS
Use any convenient handholds that will aid your progress.

PRESSURE
In most **chimneys**, you will have to use some pressure holds. Point your fingers down and press the palm of your hand against the rock at about waist level.

FEET
You do not have to find positive holds for your feet. As with **bridging** (see pp.62-63), progress can be made by **smearing** on opposite walls.

MOVING LIMBS
Ensure that you are able to maintain the pressure against both walls at all times. This is best achieved by moving just 1 limb at a time. Before moving up, get your legs as high as possible, but not above your waist.

RESTING
After a sequence of moves, lie back against the wall to release strain on your arm muscles. While **chimneying** can be strenuous, you should find plenty of opportunity to rest.

SKILL

8

TACKLING OVERHANGS

Getting over bulges in the rockface can be daunting unless you follow a straightforward plan of attack

CLEAR VIEW
Choose climbing positions where the **overhang** least restricts your vision.

BE POSITIVE
Approach **overhangs** with a determined, positive attitude.

Step 2

PULL UP

Having, as a first step, grasped the **overhang** from a **bridging** position beneath it, find higher footholds and then pull your body up onto the overhang, as you do when **mantelling**.

TECHNIQUE POINTERS
Passing an **overhang** requires a variety of techniques, depending on the situation. Because every overhang is different and every climber has his or her own style, there are no "correct" solutions.

TAKE THE STRAIN
You will find that there are various circumstances in which you can, as here, pass an **overhang** by using a mixture of **bridging** and **mantelling** (see pp.62-65), especially if it's in a corner or groove. Bridging takes your body right out from the corner, which effectively reduces the degree of bulge you have to get over and the consequent arm strain.

CHOOSING HOLDS
Overhangs are strenuous to pass. Minimize arm strain by choosing a combination of holds that reduces the degree of bulge (see "Take the Strain").

FOOTHOLDS
Support your weight on your legs for as long as possible. When reaching above the bulge, keep your heels low to stop your feet slipping.

Step 3
A LEG UP

Now that you have gained the **overhang**, treat it like a **mantelshelf**. Get your leg up (hook your heel round the shelf), as soon as possible to reduce arm strain.

SMOOTH MOVES
Plan each move in advance, then do it in one smooth movement. An **overhang** is no place to be indecisive.

• **KEEP CLOSE**
To reduce strain, keep your chest close to the rock, and resist the temptation to lean back with your head.

Step 4
OVER THE TOP

Push down with your highest leg and your hands, and straighten your arms. Use your lower leg like a counterweight, to maintain balance.

EXPOSURE
You may find that passing **overhangs** is unnerving, as you are particularly exposed both when you **bridge** or lean out below the bulge, and once you've passed it and are standing at its lip.

BEATING THE BULGE
To tackle a bulge, you may have to lean right out. Use undercut (upside-down) holds at the back of the **overhang** to hold your position, then climb as high as you can with your feet and reach for a handhold above. Get a good grip, swing out, and pull up.

PUTTING IN PRACTICE
Practise passing **overhangs** on low boulders. If you don't fall off a few times, you need to try harder!

9 ABSEILING

Definition: *A controlled descent of the rope, for a speedy descent of the rockface*

AT THE END OF A CLIMB, you may find that it is neither convenient nor possible to climb down or walk off around the side of the cliff, in which case, you will need to **abseil.** Abseiling can also be extremely useful for retreating from a **multi-pitch** climb (see pp.30-31), or when climbing on sea or canyon cliffs, where the walk there often leads you to the top of the cliffs.
Although relatively easy to master, abseiling is the one climbing activity that causes more accidents than any other. Not only is this because your security depends on a single **anchor,** but also because it is easy to become over-confident, and make mistakes.

OBJECTIVE: To use the rope safely to descend a cliff in such a way that you can retrieve the rope afterwards. *Rating* ● ● ● ●

CLASSIC ABSEIL

Classic **abseiling** *relies solely on the rope, and no other equipment. The friction needed for control is generated by wrapping the rope around your body*

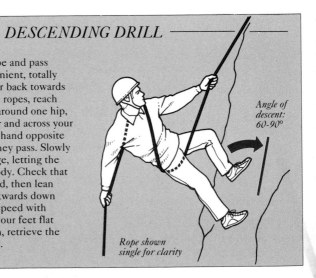

DESCENDING DRILL

WRAPPING IT UP
Find the middle of the rope and pass either side around a convenient, totally reliable **anchor.** With your back towards the edge, stand astride the ropes, reach behind and pull them up around one hip, over the opposite shoulder and across your back. Hold them with the hand opposite the shoulder over which they pass. Slowly walk backwards to the edge, letting the ropes slide around your body. Check that both ends reach the ground, then lean back and slowly walk backwards down the cliff, controlling your speed with your lower hand, placing your feet flat on the rock. At the bottom, retrieve the rope by pulling one strand.

Angle of descent: 60-90°

Rope shown single for clarity

LONG HAIR
If you have long hair or a beard, make sure it doesn't get caught under the rope. Tuck it away under your shirt collar.

UPPER HAND •
Use your upper hand to assist your balance. Resist the temptation to hold the rope tightly here, or you may get friction burns.

OBSERVATION
Keep looking at the cliff below you, and choose your route carefully.

• **LOWER HAND**
Never let go with your lower hand – it controls your speed. Move your arm forward to increase the friction and so slow yourself down.

SKILL 9

MODERN ABSEIL

*Using modern variable friction devices instead
of wrapping the rope around your body*

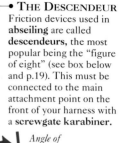

• THE DESCENDEUR
Friction devices used in **abseiling** are called **descendeurs,** the most popular being the "figure of eight" (see box below and p.19). This must be connected to the main attachment point on the front of your harness with a **screwgate karabiner.**

POSTURE •
You must lean well back, but don't let your buttocks drop below your feet, or you might find yourself doing a backward flip!

Angle of descent: 60-90°

FEET •
You don't need footholds when you are **abseiling**. Simply place your feet flat on the rockface, with your heels well down.

Rope shown single for clarity

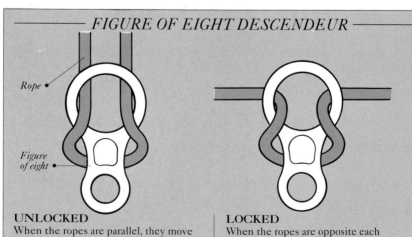

—— FIGURE OF EIGHT DESCENDEUR ——

Rope •

Figure of eight •

UNLOCKED
When the ropes are parallel, they move through the device easily.

LOCKED
When the ropes are opposite each other, they cannot move.

SAFETY
Abseiling can be spectacular and exhilarating, but don't forget that there is no one **belaying** you!

OBSERVATION •
Keep your eyes on your feet and on the route below you.

UPPER HAND •
Resist the temptation to hold the rope tightly with your upper hand.

CONTROLLING HAND •
Never let go of the rope with your lower hand. Move this hand away from your body to increase speed, and behind your back to stop.

ANGLE •
As you walk backwards down the rockface, your legs should form an angle of between 60° and 90° to the rock, so that you can push your heels into the rock.

10 MULTI-PITCH CLIMBING

Climbing on cliffs taller than the length of your rope

•

ALTHOUGH **MULTI-PITCH** CLIMBING IS, basically, like ascending several **single-pitch** climbs (see also pp.28-31), it does require a specific, structured approach. For example, in the cramped space that often exists at the end of a **pitch**, it is vital that you don't unclip from the wrong rope. You must also ensure that your ropes remain untangled.

•

OBJECTIVE: Making safe changeovers between **leader** and **second** without tangling the ropes. *Rating* ••••

•

| ——— Step 1 ——— | ——— Step 2 ——— |
| ARRIVAL | SHARING ANCHORS |

This sequence (steps 1-4) assumes that you are the **second**. When you arrive at the end of the first **pitch** of the climb, **anchor** yourself before you do anything else. Try to find a different anchor to that being used by your **leader**, and one that will resist a pull in any direction. If you cannot find a separate anchor for yourself, you will have to share the leader's.

Ignore this if you are not sharing an **anchor** with the **leader**. If you are, don't do anything to tangle the rope. The leader unclips from the anchor before you, in order to climb the next **pitch**. So that he doesn't unclip your rope by accident, ensure that your rope is below his by pushing his rope to the top of the **karabiner** when you clip in your **backline** (see below).

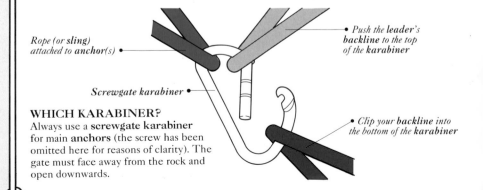

Rope (or sling) attached to anchor(s) •

• *Push the leader's* **backline** *to the top of the* **karabiner**

Screwgate karabiner •

WHICH KARABINER?
Always use a **screwgate karabiner** for main **anchors** (the screw has been omitted here for reasons of clarity). The gate must face away from the rock and open downwards.

• *Clip your* **backline** *into the bottom of the* **karabiner**

SECURITY •
On arrival at the end of a **pitch** (see Step 1), the **leader** should keep you on a **belay** until you have secured yourself to an **anchor**. The **second** must always be either anchored or belayed.

• THE SECOND'S ANCHOR
This must resist a pull in any direction. If the **leader** falls off before placing a **runner**, he will fall past you, subjecting the **anchor** to a downward pull; if after he has placed a runner, the pull will be upwards.

STAYING TIED ON
Once you've started a **multi-pitch** climb, never undo the knot connecting the climbing rope to the front of your harness until you have reached the top.

HANGING BELAYS
If there is no convenient **stance** (ledge) at the end of a **pitch**, you can **anchor** yourself to the rock and sit in your harness in order to **belay**.

Step 3

ROPE MANAGEMENT

Because you were the last person to arrive at the **stance**, your end of the rope will be on the top of the coils, and the **leader's** at the bottom (see p.41). In order to reduce the chance of a tangle, make sure that you pull all of the rope through before the leader sets off on the next **pitch** of the climb, so that his end is at the top. You must never let the rope hang down the cliff – it may snag.

Step 4

CLIMBING ON

The **leader** stays **anchored** until you **belay** him. Make sure that his rope pays out freely, and remember that the direction of force in any fall will change once he has placed a **runner**. Continue belaying him until he calls "Safe!", and remain anchored until he calls "Climb when ready!" (see pp.34-35). Before you climb, undo all knots connecting you to your anchor, and remove any **gear** from the anchor.

11

TAKING
THE LEAD

Definition: *Being the first person to ascend a* **pitch**,
without the security of a rope above you

ALTHOUGH THERE IS NO ROPE above you when you **lead**, you can
arrange some security by placing **running belays** – **anchors** where
the rope passes through the **karabiner** – at regular intervals (see
pp.78-79). Having placed these, you will still drop some distance
before the rope arrests your fall. If, for example, your nearest runner
is 2m (6½ft) below you, you will fall at least 4m (13ft). Remember –
only lead climbs that are well within your capabilities.

OBJECTIVE: Achieving security by placing **running belays**, without
also having a rope above you. *Rating* • • • • •

Step 1
SETTING OFF

On your first **lead**, climb as if there
was no rope or **protection**. Take no
unnecessary chances.

Step 2
PLACING PROTECTION

Think carefully about how you place
protection – consider your **second** as
well as yourself.

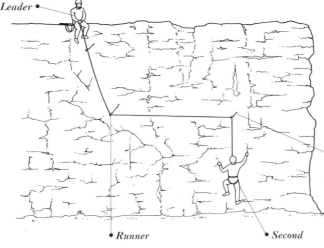

Leader •

• Runner

• Second

RUNNERS
Place however many
runners you need to
stop you from hitting
the ground. Here, a
leader falling from
near the top would hit
the ground if the top
runner were absent.

• A SAFE SECOND
If this **runner** were
absent, and the **second**
fell from this point, he
would "pendulum"
(swing from the next
runner along), and
then hit the ground.

Step 3

A MENTAL EXERCISE

As you progress, maintain absolute
concentration. Remember that
you should always climb just
as much with your eyes
and brain as with your
hands and feet.

SECURITY
Ensure that
runners are
placed firmly, in
such a way that
they cannot fall
out by accident.

ROPE DRAG
There is always the danger that a
runner may pull the climbing rope so
close to the cliff that it rubs against the
rock and so creates "rope drag". Think
about how each runner will affect the
movement of the rope, and extend it
with a short tape **sling** if necessary.

RULES FOR WIRES
Always use a short "extender" (tape
or rope loop used to lengthen a **runner**)
when placing wired **chocks** (see p.21).
This reduces the chance of them being
wobbled out of position by rope movement.
Connect the extender with a **karabiner** –
never loop it directly around the wire. Make
sure the rope passes freely through the runner,
and that all karabiner gates open downwards
and away from the rockface.

SKILL

11

PLACING RUNNERS

Finding the best positions in which to place **protection**

PRACTICE

Placing **runners** is as much an
art as a science, and requires
considerable practice. Ask
an experienced climber to
demonstrate some good
placements.

"CRUX" MOVES •

The ideal place for a
runner is as near as
possible below the
"crux" – the hardest
move of a climb. Try
to place each runner
slightly above you,
while standing on
good holds, and don't
forget that your
second is going to
have to retrieve them.

RUNNER
NUMBERS

It is up to you how
many **runners** you
place on a climb. If you
place too few and you
fall, you run the risk of
hitting the ground. If
you place too many,
you will probably
increase rope drag to
an unacceptable level.

WRONG AND RIGHT RUNNERS

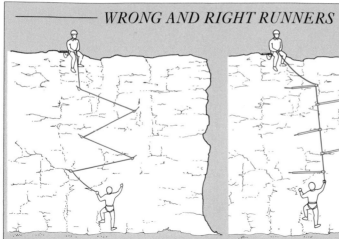

ROPE DRAG
The **runners** have caused the rope to zig-zag, which causes rope drag.

REDUCED FRICTION
By extending each **runner** with a tape **sling,** the rope runs more freely.

USING EXTENDERS •
To reduce the chance of rope drag, always extend **runners** that may pull the main rope against the rock.

WIRED CHOCKS •
Using short tape **slings** with wired **chocks** reduces the chance of them being dislodged by the movement of the main rope.

SKILL

DAY 2

12

SELF-HELP

Definition: Two simple-to-learn safety procedures

ALTHOUGH YOU MAY NEVER need them, it's wise to learn techniques that can help in certain tricky situations. For example, ascending a fixed rope to regain the rockface when you've come off, or descending to help a partner.

OBJECTIVE: To help your partner or yourself in the event of a fall.
Rating • • • • •

PRUSSIKING

A method of climbing fixed rope using friction knots that slide up the rope, but not down

—————— Step 1 ——————

TYING ON

Tie 2 **prussik loops** to the climbing rope using prussik knots (see p.25). Now attach the upper loop to the main suspension point on your harness with a **screwgate karabiner** and push this knot up until the loop is taut. With your knee slightly bent, place your foot in the lower loop and work the knot up the climbing rope so that this loop is tight.

MAKING PRUSSIK LOOPS
Make each **prussik loop** from 5mm (¼in) or 7mm (⅓in) **kernmantle** cord – fine rope – tied with double fisherman's knots (see p.25).

LOOP THE LOOP
Prussik loops must be the right length. One should run from your harness to a point up the rope that is always within reach. The second should run from one foot to a position roughly opposite your waist when your leg is slightly bent. Once adjusted, leave the loops tied and carry them with you on climbs.

• **TOP KNOT**
Tie your **prussik loops** so that the upper knot is never out of your reach.

BEWARE!
Never undo any **karabiners** or knots, especially when you're dangling after a fall!

FOOT •
Secure your foot with a "Lark's Foot": fold the rope back on itself and place your foot through both loops.

THE STEP UP

Holding the rope with a hand over, or close to, each knot, stand up in the foot loop. Stay close to the rope. Push the upper knot up as far as it will go.

IMPORTANT!
Remember, this technique must be practised before using it for real!

• TENSION
To raise the lower loop, you will need to make the rope below the lower knot taut.

• ON THE UP
Get ready to push the upper knot up. If a **prussik** knot jams, move your weight off it and twist the knot before pushing it up.

BALANCE •
Steady yourself by resting your free foot against the rockface.

• LEAN BACK
Watch the rope doesn't rub against sharp edges. If you lean back slightly, you can pull it away from potential abrasion points. Progressing both smoothly and steadily also helps.

THE SIT

Now that you have pushed the upper knot up, gently transfer your weight to your harness and sit down. You can now move the lower knot up, by making the rope below the knot taut.

THE SEQUENCE
Make progress by alternately sitting then standing, pushing each knot up the rope in turn.

ESCAPING THE SYSTEM

*Getting out of the rope **belay** system to descend and help
an injured partner – without letting the partner fall*

SKILL
12

───── Step 1 ─────
LOCK OFF

───── Step 2 ─────
FREE YOUR HANDS

Below: If your partner falls, lock the **belay** plate (see p.46). If you let go, he will fall further.

Below and below left: To escape the system, first free both your hands by tying the climbing rope around the **belay** plate with a knot (2 half hitches) so that it stays locked when you let go.

THE KNOT •
To tie the knot, pass a loop of **slack** rope through the **belay** plate **karabiner**, pull it tight, and tie (see box below).

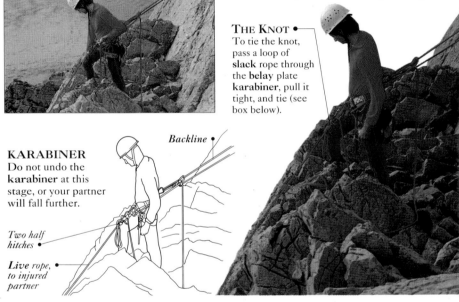

Backline •

KARABINER
Do not undo the **karabiner** at this stage, or your partner will fall further.

Two half hitches •

Live *rope,*
to injured partner

───── *TYING THE KNOT* ─────

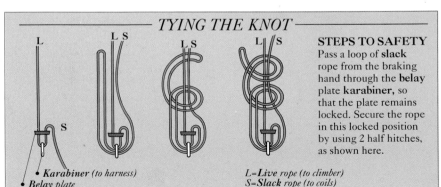

L

L S

L S

L S

S

STEPS TO SAFETY
Pass a loop of **slack** rope from the braking hand through the **belay** plate **karabiner,** so that the plate remains locked. Secure the rope in this locked position by using 2 half hitches, as shown here.

• *Karabiner (to harness)*
• *Belay plate*

L=**Live** *rope (to climber)*
S=**Slack** *rope (to coils)*

Step 3

BACK-UP

Use a **prussik loop** to form a back-up (see p.25). Tie a prussik knot around the main rope on the **live** side of the **belay** plate. Using a **screwgate** type of **karabiner** (blue in photograph), clip the other end of the prussik loop through your **backline** loop (see p.27), next to your backline karabiner.

BACKLINE •
Don't clip the **prussik loop** into your **backline karabiner**, but into the loop formed by your backline's double figure of eight knot (see pp.24 and 27).

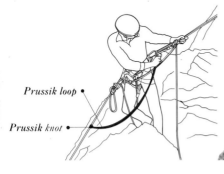

Prussik loop •

Prussik knot •

Step 4

RELEASE THE STRAIN

Reduce **slack** by pushing the **prussik loop** as far down the main rope as you can comfortably reach. Slowly undo the 2 half hitches, ensuring that you retain control of the rope through the **belay** plate. Slowly pay out the rope until the prussik loop takes the strain. Double-check the back-up, then release the rope from the belay plate.

ESCAPING
Once the **belay** plate is free, release the **backline** from your harness. Don't disturb the back-up **karabiner**. Once backed-up (see "Back-up the Back-up"), the partner's weight is on what was your backline's **anchor**, and you are free to descend the **slack** rope.

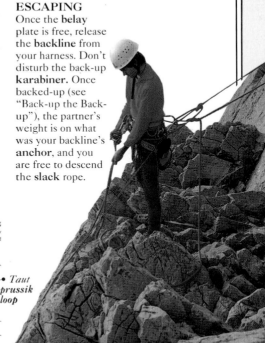

BACK-UP THE BACK-UP
Don't leave the rope secured just by the **prussik** knot. Pass a loop through the prussik **karabiner** and secure with 2 half hitches.

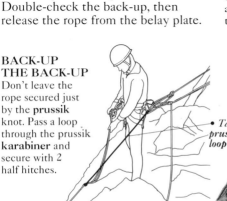

• Taut prussik loop

AFTER THE
WEEKEND

Moving on to greater things

Now that you have completed your two-day introduction to rock climbing, you may well have discovered the joys of "doing friendly battle with the rockface" and will be impatient to go out climbing again. However, this stage is, potentially, the most dangerous one, and the immediate recommendation is that you join a good climbing club (see opposite). Just because you've been shown the basics doesn't make you a competent climber – that may take several years – so don't try to climb the hard routes too soon. You'll enjoy them all the more if you wait a while.

JOINING A CLUB

MAKING CONTACT

Joining a climbing or mountaineering club has several benefits. For a start, it puts you in contact with other climbers, all of whom are potential climbing partners, and enables you to climb with, and learn from, climbers far more experienced than you. The better clubs will also have a good social life, may provide training, and will arrange regular climbing meets in different areas. Look for climbing club advertisements in specialist magazines, or try writing to the sport's representative body (see p.96).

The More You Climb ...

The more you climb, the more the bug will bite, and the more you'll want to climb – a wonderful addiction to an inexplicable pursuit. You'll experience discomfort, fear, frustration, and pain; but you will come back time and time again for the excitement, the camaraderie, and the unique adrenaline buzz of a successful ascent. And if you are extremely lucky, you may even sense a fleeting unity with your surroundings as you watch the sunset from the top of an inaccessible pinnacle.

WHERE TO CLIMB

Wherever there are rocks, there are rock climbers

ROCK CLIMBING IS AN INTERNATIONAL pastime with a growing number of devotees. Whether weekend climber, competition climber, or fully-fledged mountaineer, all agree on one thing – different areas offer different "types" of climb. Climbs on sea cliffs, for example, are totally different to those on high mountain crags. So too with climbs in canyons and disused quarries, in deep forest or open desert. Rock type and structure also affect the types of hold or degree of friction, and most keen climbers soon pick up a sprinkling of geological knowledge, even if it is only how to distinguish limestone from sandstone, or granite from slate. The following pages will give you a flavour of the wide variety of climbs enjoyed by all levels, and all nationalities, of climber – all over the world.

FRANCE

Left: The Verdon Gorge, S.E. France. Climbing in gorges has always been popular. It was in Britain, in perennially popular places like the Avon Gorge, Cheddar Gorge, and Gordale Scar, that a number of important ascents were made, several of which were hailed as the forerunners of a "new era" in rock climbing. In more recent times, it is the spectacular limestone walls of the Verdon Gorge, in France – a country where rock climbing is an extremely popular, high-profile sport – that have attracted a lot of attention and have become a magnet for all budding European rock "gymnasts".

AUSTRALIA

Below: Mount Olga, near Ayers Rock, Northern Territory. This section would be incomplete without at least a passing mention of Australia. Climbing is fast gaining popularity across this huge, ancient country, with some spectacular routes being climbed, but there is still a tremendous amount of unrealized potential and unclimbed rock.

THE ALPS
Above: Dauphiné, S.E. France. Areas like the French Alps attract thousands of climbers from all over the world each year. Remember – even if the route you wish to climb is a "rock route", you may have to cross ice or snow to get to the foot of the climb, or on your descent.

UNITED KINGDOM
Above: Borrowdale, Lake District, England. The English Lake District is regarded by many as the birthplace of modern rock climbing. Borrowdale is one of the most popular valleys, where people often queue for climbs during the height of the season. However, those willing to walk a few miles can find superb, virtually deserted, cliffs.

Left: Stanage Edge, Derbyshire, England. Climbing on "grit" – a compact, coarse-grained rock type, common throughout the English Pennines – has a particularly enthusiastic, loyal following. Gritstone rock climbing has played an extremely important part in the overall development of rock climbing. If you want to learn how to use **jamming** holds, climb on grit.

UNITED STATES OF AMERICA

Left: Yosemite Valley, Yosemite National Park, California. More of a gorge than a valley, this stunning, seven-mile ribbon, winding through high country, is surrounded by spectacular granite precipices such as El Capitan, Half Dome, and Sentinel Rock. However, this famous rock-climbing centre is not a place for beginners: the climbing is both extreme and sustained.

Above: Paria Canyon, Canyonlands, Utah. In many of the principal mountain regions around the world, rock climbing is often only considered as a sub-division of mountaineering. However, in addition to these regions, there are countless areas – such as the vast Canyonlands National Park, shown here – with low outcrops, large boulders, and old quarries, that offer virtually unlimited scope for rock climbers.

THE MOUNTAIN CODE

*Get even greater enjoyment from this rewarding sport – and ensure that
climbers in the future do too – by respecting your surroundings*

AS WITH ANY PASTIME OR SPORT, there are several extremely useful,
unofficial guidelines that are well worth bearing in mind if you
want to make the most of your climbing.

Be Prepared
Don't climb anything that is beyond your experience, and don't
climb alone. Ensure that your equipment is sound and your clothing
suitable. Learn about first aid, and check rescue call-out procedures
for your area; if visiting mountain crags,
make sure that your mountaincraft
and navigation skills are good.

Respect the Land

Keep to paths when walking through private land; only camp where you are permitted to do so. Always consider the dangers of lighting a fire; take all your litter home. When camping, dig latrines and replace the turf afterwards; avoid polluting water. Never remove or damage plants, flowers, or trees; avoid disturbing wildlife.

Consider Other People

Only **lead** climbs when you are competent to do so; respect the enjoyment of other climbers or trekkers. Never throw stones or dislodge any boulders.

Be Weatherwise

Get a local weather forecast before setting out; do not hesitate to alter your plans if the weather worsens. Only go out in snow and ice if you know exactly how to use an ice axe.

GLOSSARY

Not all these terms are used in the book, so the glossary will also help whenever you come across climbing terms elsewhere. Words in *italic* are glossary entries.

A

- **Abseil** A method of descending a rope by using friction as a control.
- **Aid climbing** Progressing up a rockface by using artificial holds such as *pitons*, *bolts*, and inserted *chocks*.
- **Anchor** See *Belay*.
- **Ascendeur** A clamp, used when *prussiking*, which slides up a rope, but not down. It is used instead of a prussik knot.

B

- **Backline** The rope from the back of a *belayer*'s harness to the *anchor* point.
- **Belay/Belaying** A belay is a point on the rock where the rope can be secured, and it is formed either by a natural rock flake, or by a piece of equipment such as a *chock*. To belay is to hold the rope in such a way that you can brake a partner's fall.
- **Bolt** An expansion bolt used as a hold, an *anchor*, or a *running belay*, fitted into a hole drilled into the rockface. Their use is considered unethical by many climbers.
- **Bouldering** Climbing (and training) on boulders and isolated, low crags.
- **Bridging** Using your body to span a corner, a *chimney*, or some other wide gap between holds.

C

- **Camming device** The *protection* devices called hexcentrics are simple camming devices because their shape means that they can be rotated to wedge into a crack. Also, see *Friend*.
- **Chalk** Magnesium carbonate, used to dry sweaty fingers and so increase grip on harder climbs. Many climbers view its use as "cheating".

- **Chimneying** Progressing up a wide crack by using various parts of your body.
- **Chock** An artificial *chockstone* designed to be inserted into a crack and used as an *anchor* or *running belay*.
- **Chockstone** A rock wedged in a crack.

D

- **Dead rope** See *Slack*.
- **Descendeur** A friction brake that is used in *abseiling*.
- **Dynamic rope** A rope that stretches when under load. Your main climbing rope must be dynamic.

E

- **Edging** Using the inner edge of the climbing boot on small footholds. "Edging boots" have special, fairly stiff soles.

F

- **Free climbing** Climbing the rock alone, without using any equipment to help make the moves. *Gear* can, however, be used for *protection*.
- **Friend/Flexible friend** A *protection* device that works by a series of "cams" – rotating parts that open out in a crack when under load, so preventing the device from pulling out.

G

- **Gear** A general term for the many *protection* devices now available. A climb with "good gear" is a well-protected climb.

H

- **Hawser-laid** A type of rope construction that uses a number of twisted strands.

J

- **Jamming** Climbing cracks by jamming parts of the body (usually fingers, hands, or fists) inside the crack.

K

- **Karabiner** (or "krab") A metal linking device, with a sprung "gate" (opening) on one side. *Screwgate* krabs have a threaded sleeve, which means the gate

can be locked shut, and this type of krab should always be used for main *belays*.
• **Kernmantle** A method of rope construction using a core ("kern") and sheath ("mantle").

L

• **Layaway** See *Layback*.
• **Layback** A climbing technique that uses the opposing forces of pulling with the hands and pushing with the feet.
• **Leader/Lead climbing** Being the first of the party to climb the route, with the rope dropping below you. *Running belays* can be placed in order to provide some protection from a fall.
• **Live** The live rope is the part of the climbing rope between the *belayer* and the climber. Also known as the "active rope". The live hand is the hand that holds the live rope.

M

• **Mantelling** A move, used to gain a *mantelshelf*, which involves changing a pull movement to a push, and getting one foot up onto the ledge.
• **Mantelshelf** An isolated ledge, or wide hold, with few other holds nearby.
• **Multi-pitch** A climb that is broken into a series of several *pitches*, because the climb is too high to be done in one standard rope length.

N

• **Nut** A general term used for any metal wedge type of *anchor*.

O

• **Overhang** Where the rock juts out beyond the vertical.
• **Overlap** A small *overhang*.

P

• **Pitch** The stretch of rockface between two consecutive *stances*.
• **Piton** A metal pin that can be driven into a crack to form an *anchor* or *runner*.
• **Protection** The means by which a *leader* secures his rope to the rock so that, if he falls, he is less likely to hit the ground.
• **Prussik loop** A loop of rope or cord that is used specifically for *prussiking*.
• **Prussiking** A way of ascending the rope by using sliding knots or *ascendeurs*.

R

• **Rack** The set of *gear* worn by a *leader*, usually in some kind of order, so that he can find any piece of equipment instantly.
• **Runner/Running Belay** An *anchor* in the middle of a *pitch*, through which the *live* rope passes.

S

• **Screwgate** See *Karabiner*.
• **Second** The second person on the climbing rope, who *belays* the *leader*, and then climbs the route afterwards.
• **Single-pitch** A route short enough to be done in a single rope length.
• **Slack** Often used in the usual way, although "slack rope" (or "inactive" or "dead" rope) also commonly refers to any part of the climbing rope not currently in use as a *backline* or *live* rope. The slack hand is the hand holding the slack rope.
• **Sling** A loop of nylon tape or rope, used to form *anchors* and *running belays*.
• **Smear** A foothold that relies on friction between the boot sole and the rock, in which as much of the boot sole as possible is pushed onto the rock.
• **Stance** A point, often a ledge, between consecutive *pitches*, where climbers regroup. A climber is *anchored* at, and *belays* from, a stance.
• **Static rope** A rope that does not stretch when under load.

T

• **Top roping** A way of securing a climb without a *leader*. The top is gained by means other than climbing, and the rope is attached to an *anchor* so that the climber can be *belayed* from the bottom of the crag. The term is also used when a climber gains the top by means other than climbing, and throws the rope down to the next climber.
• **Traversing** Moving sideways across the rockface.
• **Tying on** How a climber ties himself to the rope or to *anchors*.

W

• **Wire** A small *chock* connected to the climbing rope by a *sling* made of thin wire, rather than tape or rope.

INDEX

A

abseiling 70-3
Alpine coils, ropes 39
Alps 88
anchors:
    abseiling 70
    direct belays 49
    fixing 42-3
    multi-pitch climbs 30-1,
        74-5
    runners 76
    single-pitch climbs 29
    top belaying 48
    top roping 27
angled rock, descending 57
ankas 19
arêtes 10
ascending 54-5
Australia 87

B

backlines 27, 48
bags 9
balance:
    ascending 55
    bridging 62
    mantelling 65
bandoliers 21
barndooring 61
belaying:
    belay devices 19
    belay plates 8, 46-7, 82
    body belays 44-5
    direct belays 49
    hanging belays 75
    multi-pitch climbs 30-1
    runners 76-9
    single-pitch climbs 28
    top belays 48
    top roping 26
belts 17, 41
body belays 44-5
boots 8, 14-15
braking, belay plates 46-7
bridging 62-3, 66, 68
burns, rope 45
butterfly coils, ropes 39

C

calls 34-5
camming devices 21, 42
chalk 20
chimneys 11, 63, 66-7
chocks 21, 77, 79
chockstones 21, 66
classic abseil 70
climbing calls 34-5
clothing 12-13
clove hitch knot 25
clubs 85
code, mountain 90-1
coiling and uncoiling
    ropes 38-9
corners 10, 63
cracks 11, 58, 66-7

D

descendeurs 19, 47, 72
descending 56-7
    abseiling 70-3
    direct belays 49
    double figure of eight
        knot 24
    double fisherman's
        knot 25

E

edging 51, 59
equipment 8
    basic 18-19
    clothing 12-13
    footwear 14-15
    helmets and harnesses
        16-17
    protection 21
    ropes 22-3
    rucksacks 20
escaping the system 82-3
exposure 30, 69
extenders 77, 79

F

falls 45, 82
figure of eight
    descendeurs 19, 47, 72

figure of eight knot 24, 40
finger locks 58
flexible friends 21
footholds 51, 59
    bridging 62-3
    chimneying 67
    descending 56
    edging 51, 59
    foot jam 59
    laybacking 61
    mantelling 64
    overhangs 68
    smearing 57, 58
footwear 8, 14-15
France 87
friction devices, abseiling 72
friction knots 80-1
friends 21, 42, 43

G

glacis 11
gloves 12, 13
grading systems 32-3
gritstone climbing 88
grooves 11
guidebooks 32, 33

H

hand traversing 61
handholds 50-1, 58
    ascending 54-5
    chimneying 66-7
    descending 57
    hand jams 58, 59
harnesses 9, 17, 40-1
hawser-laid ropes 22-3
helmets 16
hexcentrics 21, 43
holds see footholds;
    handholds

I

indirect belaying 48

J

jackets 13
jammed ropes, belaying 47

jamming 58-9
jugs 51

K
karabiners 8, 19
  belaying 46-7
  escaping the system 82-3
  multi-pitch climbs 74
  top roping 27
kernmantle ropes 22-3
knots 8, 24-5
  escaping the system 82-3
  prussiking 80-1
  tying on 40

L
Lake District, England 88
lark's foot 80
layaways 60
laybacking 60-1
leaders 29, 34-5, 76-9
leading through 31
ledges 10, 64-5
legs:
  ascending 55
  descending 57
loops, prussik 80, 83
loose rocks 35

M
mantelling 10, 64-5
mountain code 90-1
mountaineer's coils, ropes 39
multi-pitch climbs 30-1,
  35, 74-5

N
noses, rockface feature 10
nut keys 21
nuts 21

O
obstacles 60-3
overhangs 11, 63, 64, 68-9
overlap 10

P
pebbles, handholds 50
pinch-grip 50
pitches 28
  climbing calls 35

pitons 21
pockets:
  footholds 51
  handholds 58
pressure holds 67
protection devices 21
prussik knot 25
prussik loops 23, 80, 83
prussiking 80-1

R
resting:
  bridging 63
  chimneying 67
ridges 10
rockface features 10-11
rocks, loose 35
rocks, protection devices
  21, 43
roofs, rockface feature 11
ropes:
  abseiling 70-3
  backlines 27
  belaying 44-7
  climbing calls 35
  coiling/uncoiling 38-9
  damage 23
  escaping the system 82-3
  knots 24-5
  multi-pitch climbs 74-5
  prussiking 80-1
  rope burns 45
  rope drag 77, 79
  top roping 26-7
  tying on 40-1
  types 22-3
routes, grading systems
  32-3
rucksacks 9, 20
runners 34
  placing 76-9
  single-pitch climbs 29

S
safety:
  abseiling 73
  climbing calls 34-5
  helmets and harnesses
    16-17
  prussiking 80-1
  ropes 38

top belaying 48
top roping 27
  tying on 40
scree 11
screwgate karabiners 19,
  46, 74
seconds 34-5, 74-5
self-help 80-3
side pulls 51
single-pitch climbs 28-9
slabs 11
slings 18, 21, 42
smearing footholds 57, 58
snap karabiners 19
socks 14, 15
static ropes 23
Sticht plates 19
storage, ropes 38
stretching exercises 63

T
tape slings 18, 42
threaded figure of eight
  knot 24
threads 42
tights 12
top belays 48
top roping 26-7, 28
trainers 8, 14, 15
traversing:
  hand 61
  low-level 52-3
trousers 13
tubers 19, 47
tying on 40-1

U
uncoiling ropes 38
undercuts, handholds 51
United Kingdom 88
United States of America 89

V
vests 12

W
walls 11
wedges 43
wire slings 21, 43
wired chocks 77, 79
wrists, mantelling 64

GETTING IN TOUCH

The British Mountaineering
Council,
Precinct Centre,
Booth Street East,
Manchester M13 9RZ

This organization is the British Isles'
representative body for rock climbing
and mountaineering. It can supply a
wide range of information, including
details of climbing clubs in your area.

ACKNOWLEDGMENTS

Kevin Walker and Dorling Kindersley would like to thank the following
for their help in the production of this book:

Richard and Helen Rodway for their modelling, and for all their time,
patience, and helpful suggestions.
John Inns and Bridget Hall, of "Crickhowell Adventure Gear" for the loan
of, and invaluable advice on, climbing clothing and equipment.
Mike Chamberlain, Warden at the Crickhowell Community Centre, for his
help with the photography sessions at the Centre's indoor climbing wall.
The staff of the Bear Hotel, the Dragon Hotel, and Mrs Lona Morgan, all
of Crickhowell, Powys, Wales, for their friendly hospitality.

Rob Gerrish and Debbie Sandersley, for assisting with the photography.
Dave Robinson, Gurinder Purewall, and Mandy Sherliker, for design
assistance; Heather Dewhurst for proof-reading; and Hilary Bird for the index.
Janos Marffy, Coral Mula, Richard Phipps, Pete Serjeant, Rob Shone, and Paul
Wilding for line drawings. Chris Lyon, for colour illustrations.
The following for the use of photographs: John Cleare/Mountain Camera (pp.6/7,
30, 84/85B, 88TL, BL & TR, 90/91); Robert Harding (pp.26 & 85TR,
photographer Robert Francis); The Image Bank (pp.86/87B, photographer Guido
Alberto Rossi, & 89BL, photographer Jeff Hunter); Wilderness Photo Library
(pp.87T, photographer John Noble, & 73TR, 89T, photographer Bill O'Connor).

A note from the author: I would like to thank all my contacts at Dorling
Kindersley for their patient help, particularly Tracy Hambleton and Ann Kay.